Guide to Successful Online Trading

[Book Edition with Audio/Video]

ISBN-13: 978-1505368437

Larry Jacobs – Editor

TABLE OF CONTENTS

Table of Contents 2

Introduction 5

Chapter 1- Swing Trading Method for Consistent Profits by Steve Wheeler 7

Chapter 2- The Astro-Trading Advantage by Tim Bost 20

Chapter 4- The Cyclical Nature of Trading by John Matteson 31

Chapter 5- Trend Following Trades Releases the New Ultimate V1 indicators for Discretionary Traders that will also be used for Automation by John Karnas 40

Chapter 6- Learn to Trade, It Is Never Too Late by Thomas Barmann 54

Chapter 7- Finding the Perfect Trade Setup By David Choe 76

Chapter 8- The EminiScalp ABL AutoTrade Strategy by Al McWhirr 81

Chapter 9- Simple and Practical Tips to Easily and Dramatically Improve Your Trading Psychology By Dr. Barry Burns 91

Chapter 10- Why do traders love Nadex Binary Options? By Gail Mercer 103

Chapter 11- A Basic, Practical and Logical Trade Strategy with Objective Entry, Stop-Loss Placement and Exit Prices By Jaime Johnson 113

Chapter 12- Multiple Time Frame Trade Strategies by Robert Miner 121

Chapter 13- Should I Trade Today? By Adrienne Toghraie 130

Chapter 14- Degrees of the Market by Sean McKissen 139

Chapter 15- Trading Stocks Using Market Profile and Auction Market Principles by Tom Alexander 144

Chapter 16- Great Tips on Buying the Right Trading Computer by Larry Jacobs 155

Chapter 17- Mastering the Emotions of Trading to Build a Peak Performance Trading Mind by Rande Howell 174

Chapter 18- Trading the FOMC Sessions with Precision by Mohan 183

Chapter 19- Links to presentations 187

Copyright..190

Disclaimer...191

About The Authors..195

INTRODUCTION

This book is dedicated to the presenters of the Traders World Online Expo #16.

This is a fascinating book that was written by over twenty trading experts.

These writers have defined strategies and have learned to profit from them. They have the ability and the conviction and discipline to act on their trading signals and make profits regardless of any outside pressures they have on them.

These traders have the attitude and use a combination of fundamental and technical analysis principles as well as psychology in their trading strategies.

Trading is one of the best ways to make money in the markets, but you need to do it correctly. You need to find the right successful trading strategies and implement them in line with your own psychology. This book will help you find the strategies that best fit you.

Again, I wish to express my appreciation to all of the writers in this book. They spent hundreds of hours of their precious time in writing their section of this book and putting together the video presentation for the online expo.

For a limited time you can access the presentations of the speakers in this book at http://www.tradersworldonlineexpo.com

Chapter 1 - Swing Trading Method for Consistent Profits by Steve Wheeler

Introduction

Let me start by introducing myself. I am a full time trader and trainer in the futures markets. I run a real time trading room four hours each trading day. I have traded for over 30 years and concentrate primarily on the currency (FOREX), crude oil, gold and stock index futures markets, such as the S & P E-mini. In a previous career, I was a practicing C.P.A. In the state of Florida.

I have developed a full suite of charts and indicators known as the Trendicators™ and 2 Market Analyzers known as the TradeFinder™ and the TrendFinder™.

What follows are the fundamental elements you need to be consistently profitable in the futures markets, using a swing trading method. I have also included information below that is crucial to your overall success in managing your risk.

Swing Trading For Profits

Swing trading implies that you are going to identify the major moves that the market makes in the timeframe in which you trade and take advantage of a portion of the major moves that are made. Market behavior tends to repeat itself over and over, so knowing these patterns can help to put the probabilities in your favor.

In terms of price behavior, a repeatable pattern is that price tends to cycle between range contraction and range expansion. After a period of market consolidation, you can expect range expansion to occur. When this range expansion occurs, you can take advantage of predictable moves that the market will make in the direction of range expansion. After entering these trades, there are logical strategies that you can employ to determine protective stop and profit target levels.

I will show you examples of price chart behavior and indicators that can best predict low risk / high reward examples.

Look at the range of the price bars on the 60 minute chart. You can see, visually, that the bar range has contracted as compared to the recent price history. The indicator on the bottom of the chart is the NaviTrader Relative ATR Indicator. You can see that the Relative ATR Indicator is at the lower range of its normal movement. When this indicator is at a low value, you will have a relatively good risk to reward ratio for your trade by placing protective stops above the recent highs or below the recent lows.

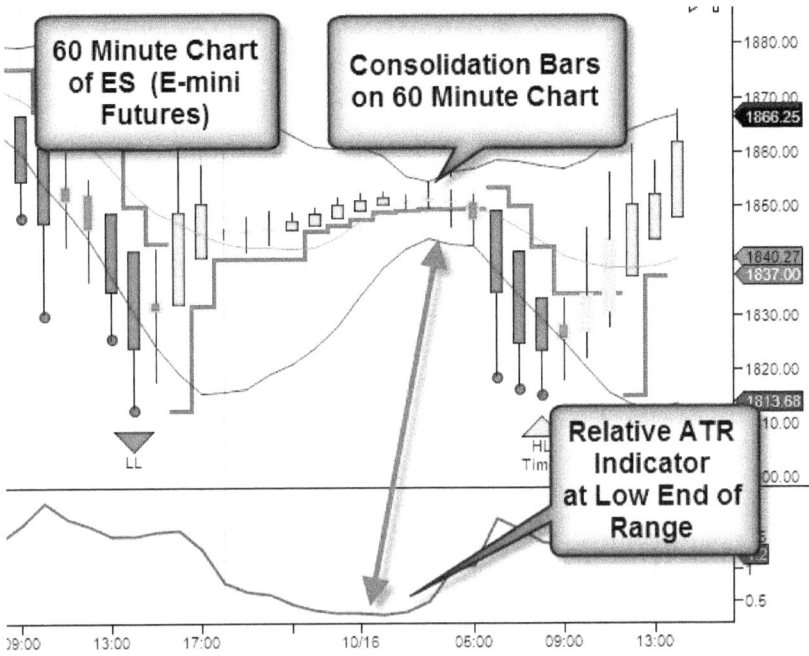

Making money in the market is a matter of being on the right side of the market. Specific to the futures markets, there are both up and down moves each day that provide many trading opportunities. One approach to the markets is to look for evidence of major support and resistance levels based on chart history. Many people ask me which time frame that I look at for my trading. My best answer is that I look at all of them. A good analogy would be that if you were going to buy or short a stock, you would most likely start by looking at a weekly or daily chart. Why would you approach the futures markets any differently? To put the odds in your favor, you must find things that occur over and over and trade with this information.

I have provided an example to the type of trade setups we look for at NaviTrader.

How To Determine The Best Market With Respect to the Risk to Reward Ratio

To determine the best markets to trade for favorable reward to risk ratios, you can scan your charts or automate the process by using a scanner, such as the Navitrader Relative ATR Scanner. You will see an example below:

Instrument			LastPrice	Navi_Relative_AT	Internal	NaviPriceConfirma	NaviHiLo
ES 12-14	Scanning For Low Relative Range		1858.50	0.825	15.64		
6A 12-14			0.8726	0.647	74.63		
6B 12-14	1.6060	1.6055	1.6059	0.529	67.99		
6C 12-14	0.8873	0.8872	0.8873	0.783	83.24		
6E 12-14	1.2807	1.2806	1.2806	0.713	76.61		
6J 12-14	0.009428	0.009427	0.009427	0.648	86.2		
6N 12-14	0.7901	0.7900	0.7900	0.652	67.49		
6S 12-14	1		1.0606	0.732	70.07		
CL 11-14	Identifying Low ATR Values in Any Time Frame		82.42	1.43	7.78		

I have listed a number of trading instruments on the scanner. The trading instruments with the lowest values will identify the trading instruments with the most favorable reward to risk ratios.

Probabilities favor the continuation of a trend. This is why you want to trade or invest in the direction of the major trend. For purposes of intraday trading or even investing, a daily chart is a very good place to start to analyze the major trend. To put the odds even further in your favor, I recommend that you analyze whatever you want to trade to find out the consistency of the trend. This can be done by measuring the trend in various time frames all the way from short term trends such as a five minute chart all the way to daily or even weekly charts.

How to Build Confidence in YOUR OWN TRADING

Preparation for trading profitably consists of market observation over a period of time so that the trader can build confidence in knowing what usually happens in the market. You will have greater confidence in your trading when you learn how to profit from the recurring market behavior that repeats itself every day. To take advantage of cycles in the markets, observe the typical move that a market moves after it moves up or down out of a range contraction pattern.

The following are observations of market behavior that will help to put the probabilities in your favor.

The real objective is to build knowledge of probabilities of market behavior so as to take consistent profits out of specific trading instruments.

One way to determine if you have this type of pattern developing is to look at the current range relative to past range. The

Navi_Relative_ATR Indicator below will indicate a relatively low value when you have a range contraction setup. The Next Chart Example:

You can take advantage of this pattern of low volatility that will predict an upcoming period of higher volatility. If the market breaks down from a period of low volatility, you will likely have a down trending market. Down trends consist of lower highs and lower lows. Up trending markets consist of higher highs and higher lows. Markets move in a wave formation, and when each wave is formed, a pivot is formed. These pivots form lower highs and lower lows in a down trend, and higher highs and higher lows in an uptrend.

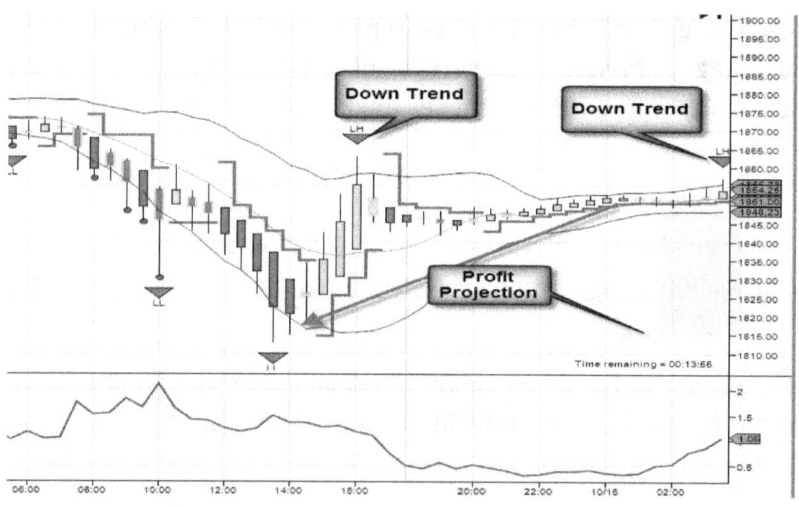

Swing Trading Method:

Chart Below is a 60 Minute Chart of the S & P E-mini:

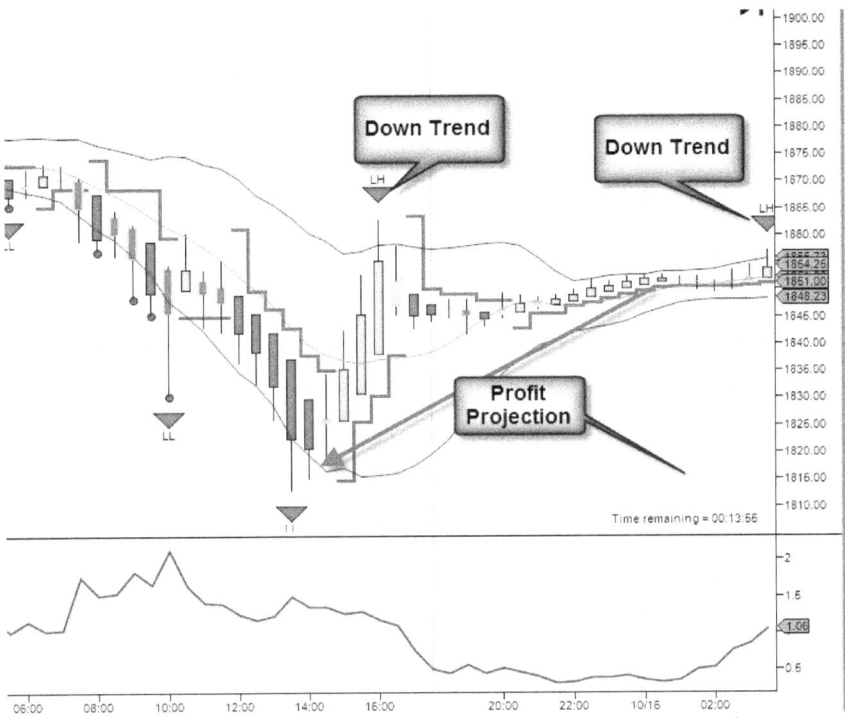

Profit Projections

Entries into the trade can be below the lows or above the highs of short range consolidation bars. The bars with the gold frames around the price are consolidation bars using the Trendicators™ charts.

Determining profit objectives for a trade exit is done by reviewing past chart history and finding recent support and resistance areas. See above chart example. The chart is in a down trend so the most likely move will be in the direction of the major trend. When price expands to the down side, a short trade can be entered, with stops just above recent resistance levels and profit projections near the recent support levels. See chart below:

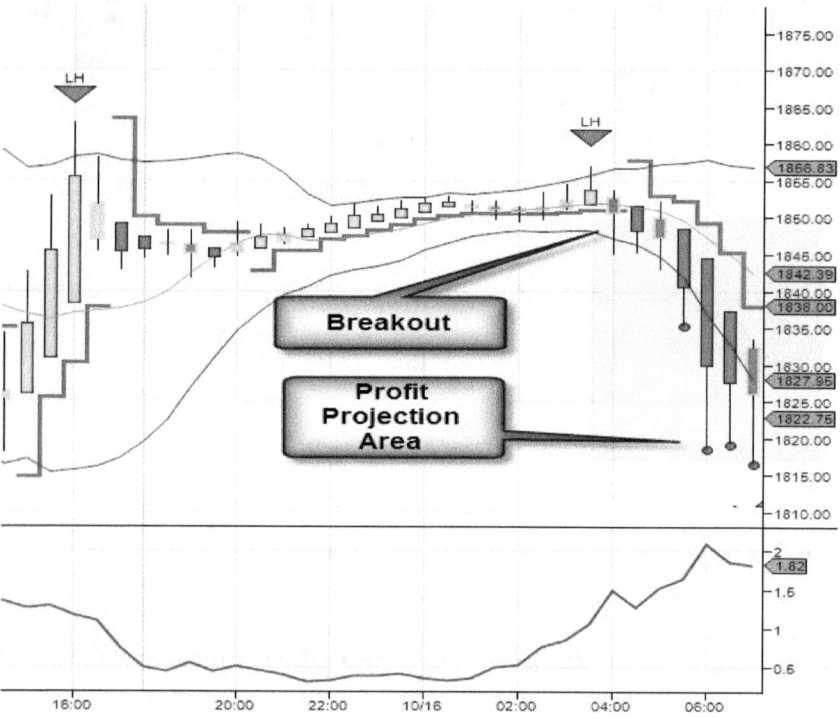

Risk Management

A primary downfall of beginning traders (as well as some seasoned traders) lies in not knowing how to manage risk or by not obeying prudent Risk Management Techniques. The use of protective stop losses (known as stops); is one important tool in trading futures. An even more important tool is known as position sizing. Position sizing answers the question of how many contracts I should trade in the futures markets as well as how many shares should I should buy or short in the stock market.

We know that trading is all about how to react to your successes as well as trades that don't go your way. No discussion of trading would be complete without a discussion of risk management. For futures trading, risk management is established with a combination of the use of stop orders combined with position sizing. You need to pair a proven strategy along with risk management. Risk management is accomplished, in general, by never taking a "big" loss on any one trade. I suggest that you start by making sure that on any one trade that you do not risk any more than one percent of your trading account. You will need to calculate before you enter a trade whether you would be risking more than one percent of your trading account.

To calculate position size you need to know some basic information such as the following:

- Account Size

- Risk Percentage that you are assuming

- Tick value of contract you are trading

- Number of ticks of your initial stop loss order

A Risk Management calculation example for the e-mini would be as follows:

a. Entry price = 1438.25
b. Initial Stop level = 1436.25 = 8 ticks on the S & P E-mini
c. 8 ticks x tick value of $12.50 = $100 $100 x 1 contract = $100 risk on this trade.
d. Account Size = $10,000

In this example, you would be able to trade 1 contract $10,000 x 1% = $100 maximum risk

Like any profession, you need to be prepared to take on the markets in a structured and methodical manner. If you study the above principles, you will better understand overall market behavior and you will be equipped to begin to consistently benefit from the great opportunities that exist each day in the markets.

Platform:

As you develop your trading skills, I suggest that you use a professional trading platform that will allow you to trade directly from the charts. The trading platform should also allow you to trade in simulation mode as well as to execute trades in your live futures account. It is important to develop your skills regarding the proper use your trading platform while in simulation mode so as to minimize trading errors after you are trading your actual trading account.

Trading in simulation mode will help you to develop your confidence and an overall methodology that fits your personality.

Developing a Belief in Your Approach and Overcoming Fear:

Most traders will develop fear as they trade due to a history of losses. Like any fear, the way to overcome it is to continue to do what you fear the most. An advantage of having a trading platform that provides for simulation is that you will be able to trade in simulation mode to build a plausible plan and to develop more confidence in your approach to trading. As you trade in simulation mode, develop a set of notes that will act as the beginning of your trading plan. Trade in simulation mode until you have mastered the use of the trading platform you have chosen. As you trade in simulation mode, practice developing the discipline needed to execute your trading plan. Through repetition, you will begin to develop into a polished and profitable trader.

Please let us know if you need any help in developing your approach to profitable trading.

Send an e-mail to mailto:support@navitrader.com with any questions and visit our website at www.navitrader.com

Above charts use the Trendicator© Charts running in the NinjaTrader platform.

Steve Wheeler
Support@navitrader.com
www.navitrader.com

RISK WARNINGS: Trading futures and foreign exchange on margin carries a high level of risk, and may not be suitable for all investors. Before deciding to trade, you should carefully consider your monetary objectives, level of experience, and risk tolerance. The possibility exists that you could sustain a loss of some or all of your deposited funds and therefore you should not speculate with capital that you cannot afford to lose. You should be aware of all the risks associated with trading and seek advice from an independent advisor if you have any doubts. Trading involves high risk and you can lose a lot of money. Trading stocks, options, ETFs, futures and foreign exchange (FOREX) carries a high level of risk, and may not be suitable for all investors. *HYPOTHETICAL PERFORMANCE RESULTS HAVE MANY INHERENT LIMITATIONS, SOME OF WHICH ARE DESCRIBED BELOW. NO REPRESENTATION IS BEING MADE THAT ANY ACCOUNT WILL OR IS LIKELY TO ACHIEVE PROFITS OR LOSSES SIMILAR TO THOSE SHOWN. IN FACT, THERE ARE FREQUENTLY SHARP DIFFERENCES BETWEEN HYPOTHETICAL PERFORMANCE

RESULTS AND THE ACTUAL RESULTS SUBSEQUENTLY ACHIEVED BY ANY PARTICULAR TRADING PROGRAM. Past returns are not indicative of future results. NaviTrader, Inc. assumes no responsibility for errors, inaccuracies or omissions in these materials. See website for terms and conditions.

Chapter 2 - The Astro-Trading Advantage by Tim Bost

We don't really know for sure.

The movements of the planets may or may not have a direct effect upon the action of prices in the markets. But with or without a proven cause-and-effect relationship, years of observation have revealed that there are clearly documented correlations between the cycles in the heavens and the kind of market trend reversals that can provide trading opportunities. So when we add an understanding of planetary cycles to our market analysis toolbox, we can gain insights and benefits that put us far ahead of most other traders.

It's the astro-trading advantage.

The Essential Ingredients of Trading Success

Astro-trading doesn't function in a vacuum. It adheres to the rules and concepts that govern success in the markets, regardless of what specific tools or methodologies we apply.

If you've been involved in the markets for any length of time you probably already understand what the key elements are that contribute to successful trading. In fact, if you don't know what those requirements are, it's almost a certainty that you haven't experienced much success in the markets. The same requirements apply to all of us as traders, but if we give them some clear attention, then we have a much greater likelihood of experiencing profitable results from our trading.

What To Trade

To begin with, of course, we have to know what to trade. The selection process will vary considerably from individual to individual. It's not a one-size-fits-all proposition. We can choose to trade equities, futures, options, Forex, or any other market vehicle that suits us personally, but in any case we have to make a decision about exactly what we are going to trade.

When To Trade

The second consideration for successful trading is knowing when to trade. For many active players in the markets, this one factor is the sole essence of trading. We not only need to know the best time to enter a trade, but also the optimum timing for exiting a position to maximize our profits or minimize our losses.

Trade Execution

While it may seem totally obvious, it's worth mentioning the fact that a knowledge of proper trade execution is also essential. Even though technology has made trading easier now than it has ever been before, we still have to be attentive to trading mechanics if we are going to be successful in the markets. Maintaining a working knowledge of trade execution mechanics is a simple thing, but if we fail to master it, all our skill at market timing instantly becomes worthless.

Psychological Management

The fourth essential component of trading success, and in all probability the most important component of all, is psychological management. It has been said, quite accurately, that trading is about 20 percent methodology and 80 percent psychology. We have to understand our own thought processes, and we must be fully aware of the things that can trip us up emotionally and psychologically, if we are going to be successful as traders.

Money Management

The final component to trading success is wise money management. The goal of this discipline is a very simple one – to be able to preserve enough of our trading capital so that we have the money we need to come back and trade again the next day. But if we don't keep our losses under control, and if we fail to preserve some of the profits from our winning trades, we will find ourselves booted out of the markets in a hurry, because all of our money will be gone. To avoid that, effective money management is essential.

The Path To Trading Success

In our practical experience as traders, we deal with each of these key components of successful trading in a variety of ways. For example, in knowing what to trade, our goal is to find a good match with our personal trading style, with the amount of trading capital that we have available, with our own individual levels of risk tolerance, and with any other factors that make a specific trading vehicle suitable to our unique needs.

We also, however, need to be aware of the fundamentals underlying the particular trading vehicle we are considering. A good understanding of market fundamentals can help us determine what to trade, so that we can reduce our risk and increase our trading leverage. Because this is the case, simply making the right choices about what to trade can make a huge difference in the results we get from the markets.

The success component of knowing when to trade is all about market timing. By using the tools of technical analysis we can improve our market timing, so that we can more easily determine exactly when to enter a trade, as well as precisely when to exit that trade for maximum benefit. Regardless of the specific technical tools that we favor as individual traders, these keys to market timing are a core part of our day-to-day engagement with the markets.

Where Does Astro-Trading Fit In?

It is within the context of market timing that the astro-trading approach is most readily applicable. When we talk about the astro-trading approach, we are speaking of the use of planetary cycle analysis as a way of enhancing our market timing. In this sense, the astro-trading approach can be seen as a sub-set of the broader field of technical analysis. It's a very specialized approach within that arena, but when we talk about astro-trading we are primarily concerned with market timing.

When we supplement our fundamental analysis of specific trading opportunities and our technical analysis of market trends with the astrological analysis that comes from studying planetary cycles, we can substantially improve our timing accuracy. Once we have used our general technical analysis tools to get a broad picture of what the specific market and trading opportunities look like, we can apply astro-trading tools to get a more precise notion of the most appropriate times for action. That's how the astro-trading advantage can enhance our market timing.

The astrological approach to the markets is effective largely because it's a correlated, but non-causal, dynamic in relation to market price history. This means that we don't base our analysis of astrological considerations on the behavior of prices during some specific interval of previous market activity. Most conventional market indicators are based on historical prices and the trends that they represent, but planetary dynamics operate outside that realm. Essentially, then, when we apply astrology to the markets we are creating an additional set of chronological coordinates that can help us fine-tune our market timing.

Mistaken Thinking

But although the astro-trading advantage gives us an extremely powerful edge as active traders, and although it can improve our profitability in the markets, the use of astrology in trading also creates myths and misunderstandings. If we want to gain the astro-trading advantage, we must be able to identify those misconceptions so that we can set them aside as we approach the markets.

First of all, it's important to get clear about what astro-trading is not. It is not voodoo, witchcraft, or the work of some kind of satanic cult. Is not about fortune telling or psychic phenomena. Is not the result of blind superstition, or of some sort of mumbo-jumbo which must forever remain incomprehensible to average traders. It's not something that is reserved for elite practitioners, since any intelligent trader can learn to use astrological dynamics to gain an advantage in the markets.

Astro-trading is not about looking at the daily horoscope column in the newspaper, and deciding whether this is a good day or a bad day to be trading. It's not about zodiac sign compatibility, or about the notion that because you are a Virgo you should only buy Capricorn stocks when you invest.

In fact, astro-trading has nothing to do with the pop culture notions that give astrology its entertainment value, making it such a great icebreaker for cocktail party conversation. As astro-traders we systematically study the repeating cycles of planetary movements and back-test their correlations with historical trends and price movements to reach high-probability conclusions about future opportunities for trading.

Unfortunately, however, once we understand what's actually involved in astro-trading, we can sometimes be seduced into believing an even bigger myth. This is the mistaken notion that astrology is some kind of magic bullet that automatically guarantees success in the markets. When we buy into this myth, we believe that all we have to do is identify a planetary event, determine its market signature, wait for the next time it takes place, and then trade at that time so we can automatically make lots of This idea that astrology gives us absolute certainty for a completely infallible edge in the markets is of course erroneous. Real astro-trading doesn't work that way. Our use of planetary cycles in the markets doesn't override regular rules of effective trading. We always combine our astrological analysis with fundamental analysis and with the tools of technical analysis as well, using it as a correlating factor to confirm wise trading decisions.

Broader Applications of the Astro-Trading Advantage

But even though astrology is not a magic bullet for traders, there is a lot more to it than many people realize. Astrology is not only an incredibly powerful asset in market timing; the astro-trading advantage can also improve our chances of proper trade execution by helping us figure out when we should not be trading at all. On top of that, the tools of astrology can also help us understand ourselves more completely, so that we can gain greater skill in the psychological management that we need for trading success.

And the application of astrology in our trading doesn't stop there. By using planetary price correlations we can discover high-probability support and resistance zones, which can help us improve our money management as well.

Figure 1 – Apple (AAPL) with Mars and Saturn support and resistance lines.

For example, in this chart showing daily bars for Apple, the operative trading channel is being defined by planetary price lines derived from the positions of Mars and Saturn. Planetary price lines are a tool that is unique to astro-trading, with the lines based on specific price correlations to the passage of planets through the degrees of the zodiac, using the techniques which are described in the book Gann Secrets Revealed Volume I: Beyond Symbolism in Financial Astrology.

If we are in a trade, we can use those planetary price lines to help us make determinations about appropriate levels for setting stop loss orders. Adding this astrological tool to our money management strategy gives us a consistent edge in protecting our trading capital while opening up a deeper understanding of the underlying forces that help drive price action and trend changes in the markets.

The Astro-Tradng Track Record

In our work at Financial Cycles Weekly during the past couple of decades, we have discovered that we can further enhance our trading results in equities and equity options by applying the astro-trading advantage to the "what to trade" question. Through an analysis of the astrological configurations associated with specific equities, we can determine in advance which stocks are most likely to experience bullish or bearish stress at a particular time in the future. After applying additional fundamental and technical filters and fine-tuning our timing projections, we share that analysis with our insider group of Gold-Plus Elite members, add the trades to our Model Portfolio, and then publish the results in our weekly newsletter.

Over a 12-year period, these combined astro-trading strategies have consistently out-performed the major market indices, as this table illustrates:

Figure 2 – Annual performance comparison of the Dow Jones Industrial Average, the S&P 500 Index, and the FinancialCyclesWeekly.com Model Portfolio, which uses astro-trading tools for stock Note that as we calculate annual performance, we re-calibrate our portfolio value at the start of each calendar year rather than using a cumulative evaluation, so that each year's trading record stands on its own. While the results have certainly varied from year to year, it's clear that using astrological tools and methodologies makes a significant difference.

This approach has been able to deliver reliable returns in bull markets and bear markets alike, bringing the kind of confidence that can only come when trading activity creates a positive outcome consistently, year after year.

And that's what the astro-trading advantage is all about!

Tim Bost
tim@timbost.com
Financial Cycles Weekly
www.FinancialCyclesWeekly.com

	DJIA	S&P 500	FinancialCyclesWeekly
2002	-16.76%	22.10%	**50.96%**
2003	25.32%	26.68%	**51.72%**
2004	3.25%	10.88%	**48.91%**
2005	-0.61%	4.91%	**14.99%**
2006	16.29%	15.79%	**9.88%**
2007	6.43%	5.49%	**17.30%**
2008	-33.84%	-37.00%	**46.33%**
2009	18.82%	26.43%	**53.30%**
2010	11.02%	15.06%	**29.15%**
2011	5.53%	0.00%	**33.65%**
2012	7.26%	13.41%	**30.35%**
2013	26.50%	29.60%	**42.62%**
Yrly Avg	5.77%	7.43%	**35.76%**

Chapter 4 - The Cyclical Nature of Trading by John Matteson

Many traders are familiar with the concept of market cycles. They understand that markets go through cycles. There will be periods when a market or instrument trends and there will be periods when they will consolidate or trade in a range. There will be times when the range expands and when it contracts. There are also cycles of profits and cycles of drawdowns. These cycles can be found in all markets and time frames.

There may be times when a market in one time frame may be trending, but at the same time, that market may be range bound in another time frame. Again, most traders are familiar with this concept, accept it and maybe even use this information to help with their trading decisions.

What many traders may not fully realize is that just as markets may be cyclical, so may be their trading systems, methods and even their performance as traders.

In this article, I hope to show you how you can identify the cycles in your trading systems, methods, etc. and then use this information to your advantage and greatly improve your trading results.

Constructing the data

First, let's see how we can construct a set of data that we can use to help identify any potential cycles. If you have a trading system or if you trade systematically, this is the obvious place to start. We simply need to collect the relevant data from each trade that you, or the system, has or would have taken. You can gather data from a backtest, forward test, your actual trades or a combination of these methods.

You will also need a way to record all these trades so as you input the data, the program will give you all of the relevant information you will need, such as win percentage, average win size vs. average loss size, maximum drawdown, net profit, etc. There are many programs available that will do this for you. If you are good with Excel, you could build your own database. I use the Market System Analyzer by Adaptrade and this works well for me by providing me with all the relevant feedback I need to do my evaluations.

In chart 1 you see I have input a series of data into the MSA program. These trades are from a forward test that I started in December of 2010. Each day, I recorded all of the trades setups that the MTPredictor software generated in the YM 3 minute time frame. I included a $5 round turn commission per contract and $5 of slippage per contract. The table to the right of the graph shows all the relevant data.

Chart 1.

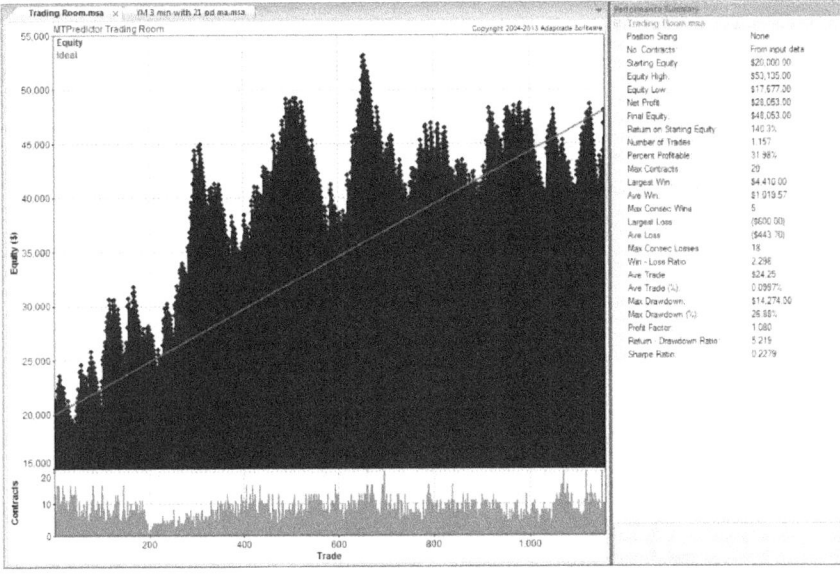

You can see these trade setups have performed fairly well over the 3 ½ year period. What I want you to take notice of, however, is the cyclical nature of the trades. You can see there are periods when the trades took the equity level to new highs and there are periods of drawdown. These peaks and troughs form our cycles. The question now becomes, how can we clarify these cycles so that they can be useful to us?

How to identify the cycle

So, how can we more clearly define these cycles so that we can first, make sense of them and later use them to improve our performance. The answer may not be as complicated as you think. All we need to do is to apply a simple moving average to our equity curve. The size of the moving average will depend on the amount of data involved. If you have less than 100 trades recorded, you will need a shorter term moving average such as a 7 period SMA. Example 2 shows the same data in chart 1 (over 1,000 trades) but I have added a 21 period moving average.

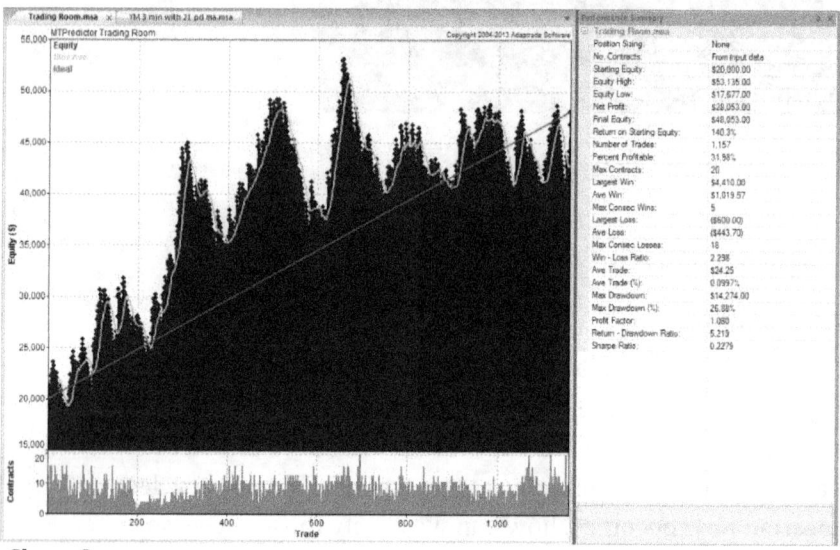

Chart 2.

Using the moving average, you can clearly see the peaks and troughs of the equity curve. Also, notice when the equity curve (in blue) moves above the moving average (green line), it tends to signal a good cycle of trades is ahead while just the opposite is true when the equity curve drops below the moving average. When this happens, the trades tend to take the system into a drawdown. Hopefully, you can see how this information might be useful. If not, read on.

Using the cycles to improve performance

Once you identify the cycles, as determined by the moving average, you can now identify when your method or system is in a good cycle, which should produce an overall series of profitable trades, and when it is in a drawdown or negative cycle which, we expect to result in a negative series of trades.

What if you only traded your method or system when the equity curve closed above the moving average and stopped trading that method or system once the equity curve clearly closed below the moving average? This would allow you to trade when your system is in a good potential cycle and avoid it when it is potentially heading into a drawdown.

Chart 3 shows trades taken only after the equity curve has closed above the moving average. You can see how this equity curve is much smoother. You can also see how this has not only improved the overall profit, from a 140% return in the raw data from Chart 1 with a maximum drawdown of 27%, to a return of over 390% with a maximum drawdown of only 9% when the moving average is used to determine when to trade and when not to trade.

Chart 3.

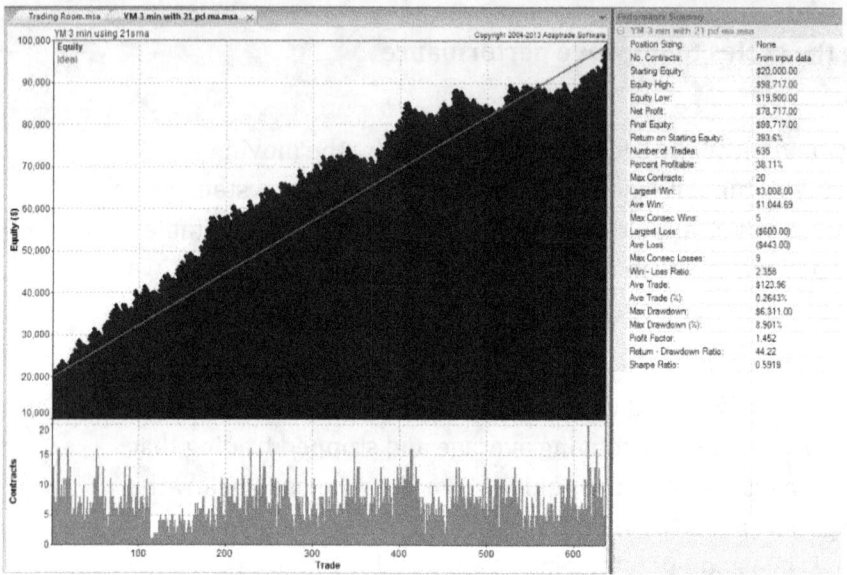

It should be clear how this can improve your performance or the performance of your system or method. Perhaps, even more importantly, it will stop you from trading a system once it closes below the moving average. This is extremely important because the system may never close back above the moving average again! This frequently happens as some systems may work in certain types of markets but fail in others. Without knowing when you or your method/system has entered a potential drawdown, you may continue to trade while your system goes into a death spiral and takes your account balance with it!

Additional applications

There are many different ways one can approach this as well as many different applications. For example, the same method or system may be profitable during a 30 day period when using a 5 minute time frame, but unprofitable when a 3 minute chart is used. This may be due to the fact that each time frame has its own cycles of productive periods and unproductive periods. Each market may also have its own cycles so, for example, the cycles in oil using a trading system, may be different than the cycles in the Dow. How can we use this information? What if you knew the cycles for your method or system in multiple markets? What if you only traded a market when a productive cycle was anticipated? Once that productive cycle came to an end, you would stop trading that market and begin trading another market that was now anticipated to be entering into a productive cycle.

For example, Let's say that you have been trading the Dow using your method or system on a 3 minute chart during a productive period. That period has now come to an end as the equity curve has closed below the moving average. Around this time, you observe that the oil equity curve in the 5 minute time frame has closed above its moving average and you now anticipate that it will begin a productive and profitable cycle, At this point you would stop trading the Dow and start trading oil. This can potentially have the benefit of allowing you to always be trading the right market at the right time.

Final analysis

Hopefully, you can see the potential benefits of being able to identity the cycles in your trading and only trading when you anticipate a good cycle of trades is about to unfold, and to stop trading when the productive run has come to an end. In many cases, you will see how this can greatly enhance the results of your system or method.

You may find that using the equity curve and moving average actually decreases the return of your strategy but cuts the maximum drawdown in half. This allows you to be able to make the decision if it is worth giving up a few percentage points of return for a smaller drawdown. In many cases, it will not only increase profits over time, but also reduce the size of the maximum drawdown.

This article is only meant to be food for thought or a starting point for you to explore further on your own. Hopefully, I have pointed you in the right direction to begin your own journey to better trading results!

John Matteson
scalpersgold@yahoo.com

MTPredictor
www.mtpredictor.us

Chapter 5 - Trend Following Trades Releases the New Ultimate V1 indicators for Discretionary Traders that will also be used for Automation by John Karnas

Trend Following Trades Releases the New UltimateV1 Indicators for Discretionary Traders that will also be Used for Automation

This article will be going over the new TFTUltimateV1 indicator set from Trend Following Trades that can either be used on a chart, with the patented TFT AMA or with both. They will also be the core of the upcoming TFT Automation Strategies. Once we go over all of the indicators and their new advanced features we will then discuss briefly how TFT will deploy automation and what we will do to help insure their initial and long term success.

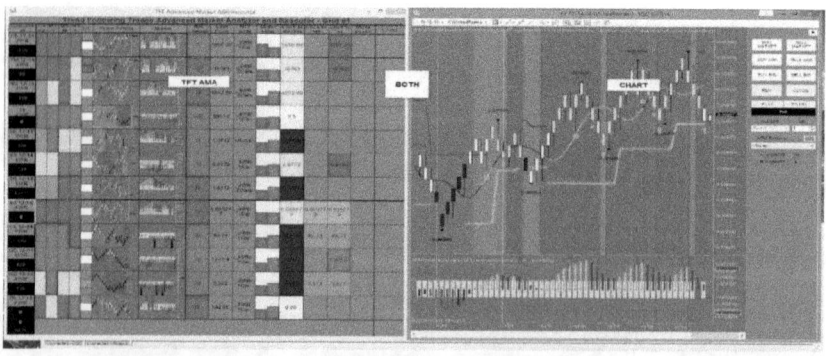

Here at Trend Following Trades, we have been trading a very visually simplistic trend following method with great success. Our visually simplistic method allows for traders to make trading decisions based on an Indicator and Rule Set that doesn't "clutter up" the chart with many indicators that have to come into alignment in order to take high probability Trend Following Trades. The TFT Method works the same EXACT way regardless if you're intra-day, swing or position trading of Futures, Forex, Stocks, ETF's or Options on them.

Although many other "complicated" Methods may have decent individual performance, often trades are missed because of having to look at so much information, real-time, which leads to "decision lock", causing traders to miss good, valid trades as well as feeling like they have to take lower probability trades, late in the swing move. Also, not to mention what it would take (from a screen real-estate standpoint) to monitor and trade MANY markets!

We've also taken this VERY robust, back testable TFT Method, with great results, and brought it into a "Grid" type of trading Platform that integrates seamlessly with NinjaTrader 7. This is called the Trend Following Trades Advanced Market Administrator (TFT AMA). This is a patented product being shown using NinjaTrader 7.

We now have filters that keep us out of Non-Trending Markets, and now we no longer need to wait for the few markets that we may have been monitoring with individual charts, to begin trending or try and force trades that don't have the highest probability of success in the few markets that we used to look at. You can now trade up to 12 markets all on one monitor! You can, also, have multiple AMA's running (up to 5), only being restricted by computer hardware limitations (number of monitors, CPU power and amount of memory). You can watch Futures, Stocks and Forex markets all at the same time, depending on which versions of the AMA you have purchased.

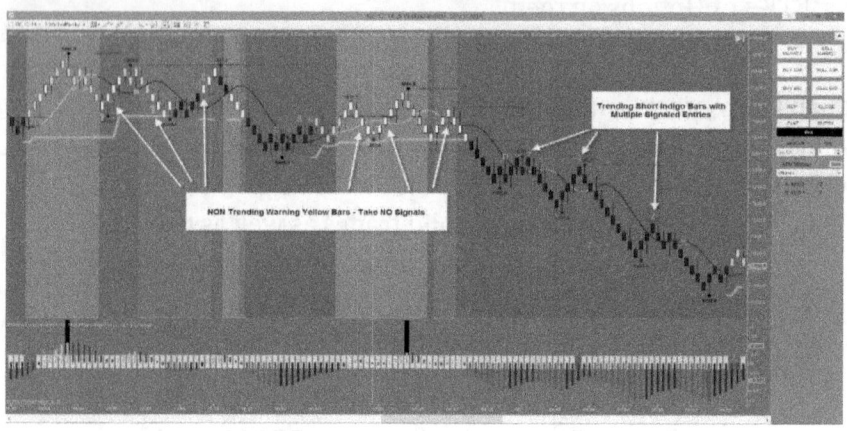

The TFT AMA is FAR more than just a Market Analyzer, it is a complete Market Administrator. It has many Market Analyzer functionalities, but also incorporates single click trade execution (with automatic price calculation of entry BEFORE trades trigger) and money management functionality, according to the TFT Chart Method and its Set-ups and trades. Along with this, is the ability to EASILY identify early trend indication, Short-Medium and Long Term market structure and conditions of divergence, ALL with a visually simplistic and easy to understand coloring of cells in the

TFT AMA, either Green for Bullish or Red for Bearish conditions (also light Green and Red for early notifications of these conditions).

The TFT AMA is designed to be used on half of a 1080P monitor (if you only have one), of any size, which will allow you to have charts up along side of the AMA for traditional chart viewing of the TFT Standard Enhanced Chart method OR some other charts and other indicators that traders may feel valuable placed on any chart. Left side support and resistance identification of the market being traded can also be picked up looking at these charts. The TFT AMA can also be maximized on one monitor and charts can be pulled up on a second, third, etc. monitors, if desired.

Once placed next to charts, you can click on the far left hand side cell of the TFT AMA (the one that shows the market and time frame) and the chart or charts of that market will immediately appear on the other side of the screen. If you are using NinjaTrader's Chart Trader, then all orders, stops and targets can be shown, manipulated there, AND/OR on a DOM that is located on another monitor. There is no longer the need for multiple time frame charts as the Market Structure cells (Middle and Long term) will show the longer term picture of Market Structure, that is often used as a filter to only take trades in the direction of the larger trend, on secondary, longer time frame charts (see chart at top of next page) ----->>>>

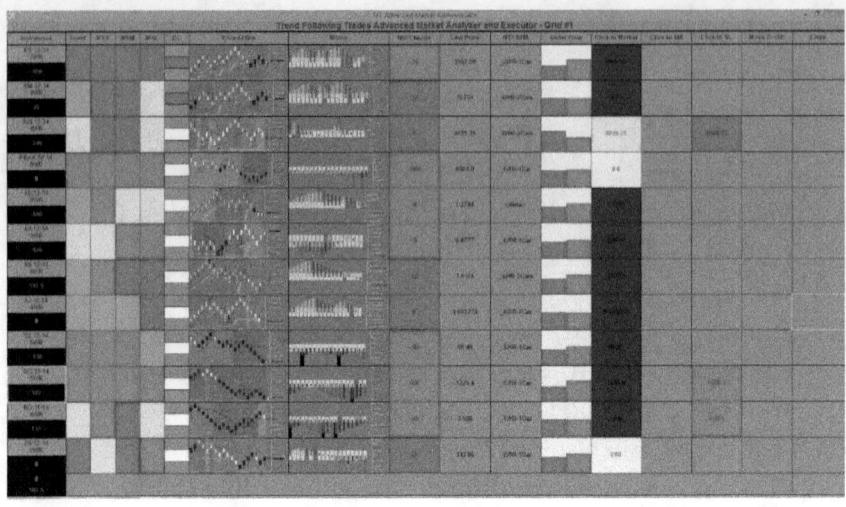

Once an order is placed, the TFT AMA will automatically use a pre-selected NinjaTrader 7 ATM, cancel and resubmit the Stop Market or Stop Limit orders to a better price, if not triggered in on the current bar, the TFT AMA will give you the ability for a better price entry. Once that order is automatically re-submitted and the market continues to move away from the intended direction of the trade trigger, without triggering in, then the order will automatically be cancelled for good, for that particular set-up. Essentially making the TFT AMA a manual Auto Trader of the TFT Method! If there is no set-up warning on the AMA, then there is NO chance of taking a non Method or non planned trade, unless you decide to Market in by left clicking on the Market Order Cell OR right clicking on it for entry into the market, in the opposite direction (for those that chose to counter trend trade from the TFT AMA).

The most unique items of the TFT AMA are the Price Action and Momo Cells. These cells show a real-time condensed area of Panel 1 price and Panel 2 TFT Momo area of the Chart (there is an input for choosing the number of past bars you chose to see). This enables you to actually see real-time, price movement and the TFT Momo indicator (and whatever else you have in Panel 1 and Panel 2) without ever having to pull up or look at a chart. This technology works for charts that aren't even being displayed on ANY monitor. This functionality allows Traders to see what's happening in up to 12 markets on Panel 1 and Panel 2 of a chart without having to have ANY charts being displayed!

The TFT AMA also has individual market close and move to break even cells. If a trade is in profit and at a point that you wish to remove the risk out of the trade, simply click on the orange break even cell and the stop will automatically be moved to break even. If at ANYTIME you wish to exit the entire position, simply click on the close cell of the market that the position is in, and it will exit the position immediately (whether it's in profit or loss).

These functionalities are designed to be used to override any NinjaTrader 7 ATM's that are assigned and being used in any particular trade (i.e. if a double top, double bottom, area of support or resistance is being approached, before your first target, you can easily make in trade exit or money management decisions, right in the TFT AMA)!

Also displayed in the far left, Market Type and Time Frame cell, is the open and closed profit and loss for that trading session (very similar to what NinjaTrader 7 displays). The last row displays Global profit and loss, showing real-time open and closed profit and loss. If at any time you are in single or multiple positions and you decide that you want to exit ALL positions, the Global lower right hand close cell can be clicked on to immediately exit out of all positions (i.e. if you are at your daily target or stop loss, you can use this cell to go flat and be done trading).

We have also added an Order Flow cell to the TFT AMA. This cell shows a percentage ratio between contracts that are being executed at the bid versus the ask, back to the last swing point of your choice (short, middle or long). This type of "Cumulative Delta" Swing Order Flow, helps traders to determine whether a pullback into the TFT "Value Area" is simply profit taking OR if Traders are actually initiating larger positions opposite to the current swing (i.e if looking to go short, you may want to make sure that the red bar on the Order Flow cell is higher than the green bar). This simple yet powerful tool addresses what we consider to be the last form of volume that still has trading decision validity. As an owner of any version of the TFT AMA, you can also color your trigger line either cyan for net long or indigo for net short, on the chart. The massive amount of High Frequency Trading Volume or "Black Box" Algorithms have really disrupted the reading of standard up and down volume of each price bar and even daily cumulative delta volume, so now we're looking at the most recent swing, cumulative delta volume, which we are calling "order flow".

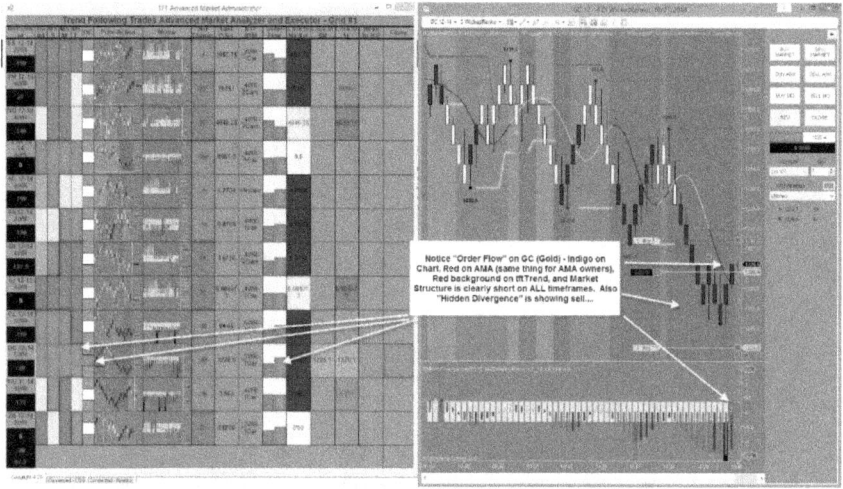

Trend Following Trades has always been about trading from the inside and out (meaning not picking tops and bottoms, trading the middle part of a move or for those Elliott wave theorists, trading wave 3). The problem with simplicity on a chart is while giving the trader the best chance of not running into "decision lock". For experienced traders this is not a big problem, because they will simply draw in line of support and resistance, draw in lines of different type's divergence on whatever indicators that they are using, looking at credible volume, like cumulative delta volume, etc. The problem with this is that it still takes time, focus, expertise and a keen eye to be able to do this successfully with more than one market simultaneously. The TFT UltimateV1 indicators were designed to assist the discretionary trader and provide the basis of which the TFT Automation Strategies are being written.

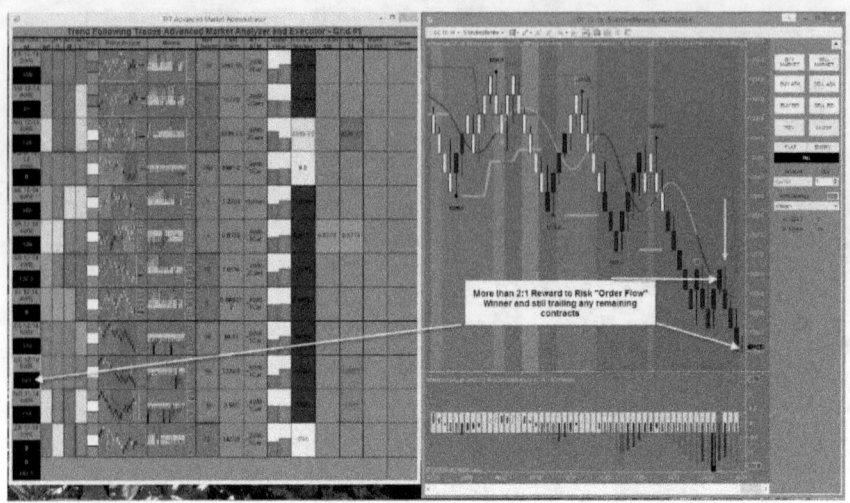

The TFT UltimateV1 indicators now also feeds the TFT AMA giving the trader the ultimate edge in trading.

Saving the best for last, we finally get to discuss strategy trading (automation). This is something that we have been talking about for almost 2 years and have had many people try to convince us to automate immediately, when we first started talking about it. I didn't feel comfortable doing this because I didn't feel that the indicators programmed close enough to a point where they could be coded mathematically. With this latest release, we have successfully coded over 90% of what is currently being used by our best discretionary traders and have provided around 70% of those indicators in the TFTUltimateV1 package for discretionary traders.

We are firm believers now that successful strategy trading, over a long period of time, requires a few absolute necessities regardless of the method/strategy being traded. Please see our requirements, in order of importance below:

1) The strategy that you are trading can NOT be curve fitted or optimized with data from the last 12 months of trading.

2) You can NOT allow too much size to be traded at the same computer time, same price level, same direction and in the same market.

3) Although scalping can be fun, it doesn't make for what I consider to be a good growth plan of income when increasing size during intra-day trading. Trying to trade 10-20 contracts for less than 10-20 ticks (with a reward to risk range in the 2:1 area) we consider to be an exercise in futility once you take commission and real money fills, into account, at that size level.

4) With the cost of leasing collocated hardware as part of an intranet (in the same building), instead of a home computer/office computer hooked up to the internet (no matter how fast either office/home set up is), your   execution time to the global matching exchange engines can be less than   1 millisecond as compared to around 30-50 milliseconds (with the best internet and computer office/home hardware). Since over 70% of the Futures volume is now estimated to be provided by computers, who really thinks that they can run a strategy, in an office or home

environment, successfully against collocated hardware, no matter how good the strategy performs in a back test?

5) Trend Following Trades believes that automation is something that should   enhance and improve the performance of a discretionary method. The worst thing that I have seen is companies selling strategies that a) have no   real limitations built into them from a trading size standpoint, b) take trades without at least better than a 75% knowledge from looking at a chart that it's taking trades from, when, where and if it should be taking   those trades and where it's targets and stops should be.

6) TFT believes that large amounts of protection should be built into the strategy in case of unexpected market price action that could destroy one's account very quickly.

7) Have your broker trade the strategy on a collocated computer in the Futures market - they have all the tools and account access to do whatever is necessary to get out of trades should things go haywire. TFT's strategies   will have auto shutoff functions built into them should the markets go crazy   but if the strategies get disconnected and your position needs to be flatted, then they can do it immediately.

8) Last but not least, we believe that every strategy should be monitored by a human being via remote monitoring software (Windows Remote Desktop, Teamviewer, etc.) - if the software is being run by the trader on a remote   computer, so that the

trader with knowledge of what the strategy should be doing or not doing can turn it off quickly, if need be. This will only come into play if TFT can find an unbreakable secure way to limit the TFT method, for traders use in the Forex and Stock markets, who wish to do this. This may present to be too monumental of a task, which we won't know until we go to protect a Forex or Stocks live strategy. If, we find a way to do this, we don't believe in "run it and go golfing mentality", it's more so about using computers to do what we traders do the worst: a) trade with emotion computers do what they are told to do, not what they want to do or what they think they should do, just what they are told to do (unless of course there is a problem, which is why we monitor the strategies, so we can turn them off, if something is wrong)………HOPEFULLY! (keep your brokers number in your cell phone ready to dial the trade desk just in case) b) are slow at executing trades (compared to a computer).

If you have any further interest in finding out about what is discussed above, please do not hesitate to email us at info@trendfollowingtrades.com and/or visit us at www.trendfollowingtrades.com or call you can call us at (215)-909-9617 usually between the hours of 1PM and 7PM US EST. We are real money traders ourselves and are generally not finished trading until 1PM EST. We will not take phone calls until we are finished trading (once our daily target or stop is achieved or if the market is cooperating nicely then we will trade into the close).

John Karnas
john.karnas@verizon.net

Trend Following Trades, LLC.
Trendfollowingtrades.com

U.S. Government Required Disclaimer - Commodity Futures Trading Commissions Futures and Options trading has large potential rewards, but also large potential risk. You must be aware of the risks and be willing to accept them in order to invest in the futures and options markets. Do not trade with money you cannot afford to lose. This is neither a solicitation nor an offer to Buy/Sell futures, options or ANY sort of chartable instrument. No representation is being made that any account will or is likely to achieve profits or losses similar to those discussed on this web site. The past performance of any trading system or methodology is not necessarily indicative of future results.

CFTC RULE 4.41 - HYPOTHETICAL OR SIMULATED PERFORMANCE RESULTS HAVE CERTAIN LIMITATIONS. UNLIKE AN ACTUAL PERFORMANCE RECORD, SIMULATED RESULTS DO NOT REPRESENT ACTUAL TRADING. ALSO, SINCE THE TRADES HAVE NOT BEEN EXECUTED, THE RESULTS MAY HAVE UNDER-OR-OVER COMPENSATED FOR THE IMPACT, IF ANY, OF CERTAIN MARKET FACTORS, SUCH AS LACK OF LIQUIDITY. SIMULATED TRADING PROGRAMS IN GENERAL ARE ALSO SUBJECT TO THE FACT THAT THEY ARE DESIGNED WITH THE BENEFIT OF HINDSIGHT. NO REPRESENTATION IS BEING MADE THAT ANY ACCOUNT WILL OR IS LIKELY TO ACHIEVE PROFIT OR LOSSES SIMILAR TO THOSE SHOWN.

Use of any of this information is entirely at your own risk, for which TrendFollowingTrades.com, its affiliates, employees or owners will not be liable. Neither we nor any third parties provide any warranty or guarantee as to the accuracy, timeliness, performance, completeness, or suitability of the information and content found or offered in the material for any particular purpose. You acknowledge that such information and materials may contain inaccuracies or errors and we expressly exclude liability for any such inaccuracies or errors to the fullest extent permitted by law. All information exists for nothing other than general educational purposes. We are not registered trading advisors.

Chapter 6 - Learn to Trade, It Is Never Too Late by Thomas Barmann

In general, we differentiate three types of investors or traders:

Long-Term Investor: Focusing on buy and hold, making money when asset prices rise; working mostly with fundamental analysis; on the search for assets with a higher performance expectation. Positions are held for weeks, months, and years.

Swing Trader: Trading with short-term money moves of selected assets, based on technical- or fundamental analysis. Asset positions are held for multiple days or weeks.

Day Trader: Positions are opened and closes at the same day. Rarely is a position carried overnight; in particular on stocks, preventing gap risks, while futures trade more or less 24-hours a day.

Are traders or investors better on in the long-run?

To answer this question, we measure the return expectations for stock trades/investments.

Our models are based on institutional money flow. Table-1 shows institutional market drivers and followers per key market segment.

Table1: Institutional Investors

Financial Markets	Drivers	Focus
Stock Market	Prop traders, seeking best performers	Fund managers, measuring themselves relative to market indexes: Dow, S&P 500, NASDAQ, Russell 3000
Currencies	Prop Traders Federal Banks	Over the counter (OTC) deals, where one institution interacts with another in support of the international exchange of goods, paid in various currencies.
Treasuries	Prop Traders	Banks, hedging their lending.
Commodities	Prop Traders	Producers and industrial consumers, hedging for constant purchase and sell prices.

When institutional money starts flowing in or out of an asset, the average expected price move of the share value in the next 1-5 days is about 1.8%. Taking a long-term perspective from a weekly chart, a 3.5% price move in the next 1-5 weeks can be expected. Those, who open and close positions at the same day, achieve about a 0.6% price move with the average stock. Calculating the median-time for staying in a trade, we came to three bars, this means:

Long-term Investing: 3.5%-return on capital engaged in three weeks.

Swing Trading: 1.8%-return in three days.

Day Trading: 0.6%-return in about 3 hours.

For our calculations, we assume a high probability trading system, giving you two wins out of three trades:

Graph-1: AAPL Daily NeverLossTrading HF Chart

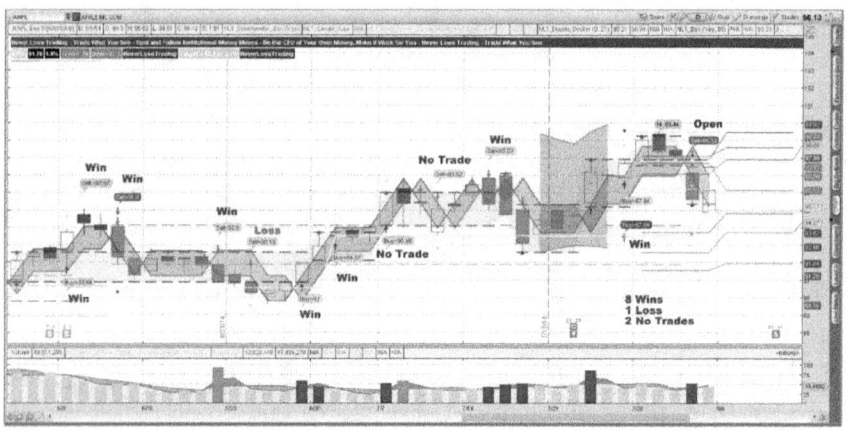

In addition, let us assume a 1:1 reward/risk setup for each trade.

Based on those assumptions we compare the return expectation of the three different traders/investors; calculating the upper part of table-2 cash based, applying a 2:1 margin for swing traders and long-term investors and a 4:1 margin for day traders:

Table-2: Return and Risk Expectation of Different Investors

Without Margin	Probability for Success	Expected Price Move after Institutional Engagement	Average Time to Reinvest (trading days)	Capital Turns in Three Weeks	Expected Thee Week Return (w/o commissions)	Expected Risk per Trade	Return on Risk
Long-Term	66%	3.5%	15	1	2.3%	3.5%	66%
Swing Trader	66%	1.8%	3	5	5.9%	1.8%	330%
Day Trader	66%	0.6%	1	15	5.9%	0.6%	990%

Using Margin	Probability for Success	Expected Price Move after Institutional Engagement	Average Time to Reinvest (trading days)	Capital Turns in Three Weeks	Expected Thee Week Return (w/o commissions)	Expected Risk per Trade	Return on Risk
Long-Term	66%	6.8%	15	1	4.5%	6.8%	66%
Swing Trader	66%	3.4%	3	5	11.2%	3.4%	330%
Day Trader	66%	2.0%	1	15	19.8%	2.0%	990%

The two calculations shows that the day trader, when using margin can expect the highest return and is risking the least amount of money per trade, while the long-term investor is taking a risk above the average expected return. Swing Traders in both examples have a positive expectation between risk and reward.

Why do so many people prefer long-term investing?

Our answer: This is what you been thought investing in; thus you prefer long-term holding of Mutual funds, 401(k), and broker held assets or ETF's. When you hold assets for the long-term, you allow for the institution of your brokerage account to sell call options against your assets, giving them an average return of about 1% per month that you never see in your account.

If you want to make a change to this, there is only one way, learn to trade, it is never too late:

Regardless if you are a fulltime or part time trader, make trading your own business and take it serious. Unfortunately, many new traders feel they can make a lot of money in the financial markets with little knowledge and little engagement. However, the best way to trading success is to replicate the setup of a professional trader, working at an institution, where they have their support- and control network, assisting them to strive for success.

One way or the other, build a base to replicate such network, either on your own or by engaging in a premier trading education institution like NeverLossTrading. Here are the key components for your trading success:

Component-1: Trading System

Without a reliable system, which constantly gives you clearly defined entries, exits, stops, and odds evaluations, trading success is rather random and mostly inexistent.

In general, we find three types of trading systems and compare them based on measured probabilities for success, resulting in an average expected return rate.

Moving Average Based Systems take their trade entry comparing longer- and shorter-term price happenings from the past and initiate an entry when the longer- and shorter-term component of the observation are crossing.

Prediction Based Systems assume that longer-term price patterns repeat themselves and thus allow the trader/investor to follow them.

Activity Based Trading Systems analyze short-term changes in supply and demand patterns, indicating the setup of a potential directional price move.

In the first example, the systems are compared on cash investments into stocks. The dynamic and impact of using leveraged instruments like options or Futures, brings referring higher outcomes. All results published are based on years of statistical materials and 30 years of trading with many different models.

The following example shows that the average trader can expect a .300-percen favorable outcome, when using a high probability and activity based trading system.

Table-3: Trading Systems Compared

Systems	Moving Average Based	Prediction Based	Activity Based
Examples	MACD, Bollinger Bands, Stochastic, RSI, Moving Averages	Elliott Wave, Gann Square, Trade Patterns	Short-Term Changes in Supply and Demand
Decision Base	Price/Line Crossings	Conclusions: D follows A, B, C	The Crowd Follows the Leaders
Accessibility	Standard Indicators or Slightly Modified Versions, Available in Most Trading Platforms	Individual or Program Based Assumptions to be Applied to Individual Trade Setups	Algorithmic Based Trading Systems, Running on Own or Open Programmable Trading Platforms
Average Trade Setup Probability	53% - 55%	53% - 57%	> 65%
Mid-Level	54%	55.0%	1

Aside from the return expectation, the average costs of a trading system are a key consideration. Let us compare those and the payback cycle for a stock trader using $50k with margin or $100k in cash. We further add a Futures Trader, using $10,000 in cash, applying one-quarter of day margin.

Table-4: Return On Investment Calculation: Stock Trader and Futures Trader

Return on Tuition	Moving Average Based	Prediction Based	Activity Based
Education Packages	$500 - $5000	$2,000 - $5,000	$5,000 - $15,000
Median Price	$1,000	$2,500	$10,000
Annual Cash Return Expectation for Stock Investments, Considering 1%-Slippage, Including Commissions			
A) Long-Term Investor	3.5%	4.7%	18%
B) Swing Trader	9.0%	12.0%	45%
C) Day Trader	9.0%	13.5%	45%
Applied Formula: Return =((Probability for success - 1% slippage)*Return Expectation*Capital Turns) - (Probability of Failure)*Risk*Turns)/Capital			
Stock Trader Return on $50k Margin or $100k Cash			
First Year Return			
A) Long-Term Investor	$2,500	$2,000	$7,500
B) Swing Trader	$8,000	$9,500	$35,000
C) Day Trader	$8,000	$10,500	$35,000
Second Year Return			
A) Long-Term Investor	$3,500	$4,667	$17,500
B) Swing Trader	$9,000	$12,000	$45,000
C) Day Trader	$9,000	$13,500	$45,000
Futures Trader Return on $10k with 1/4-Day Trading Margin			
First Year Return			
A) Long-Term Investor	$2,500	$2,167	$7,500
B) Swing Trader	$8,000	$9,500	$35,000
C) Day Trader	$9,500	$11,500	$42,500
Second Year Return			
A) Long-Term Investor	$3,500	$4,667	$17,500
B) Swing Trader	$9,000	$12,000	$45,000
C) Day Trader	$10,500	$14,000	$52,500

The first year calculation includes the recuperation of the initial tuition costs.

For both traders, you see that activity based trading systems; even so they ask for a higher initial investment, produces returns far beyond moving average- or prediction based systems.

Let us take the NeverLossTrading Top-Line System as an example for an activity based high probability system.

The system spots changes in supply and demand, initiated by institutional leaders, mostly Prop Traders. At the instance, when other market participants recognize their engagement and jump on the band wagon, the NLT Top-Line User trades with a defined entry-price-threshold, a defined target, and stop; always considering that the odds remain in favor of the trader.

Market makers are the key gate keepers; they immediately recognize and react on changes in supply or demand, conducting a price change, often combined with a volume change. This triggers the potential trade alert, when it is acknowledged, you enter into a trade considering:

Graph-2: NeverLossTrading Supply and Demand Model Base

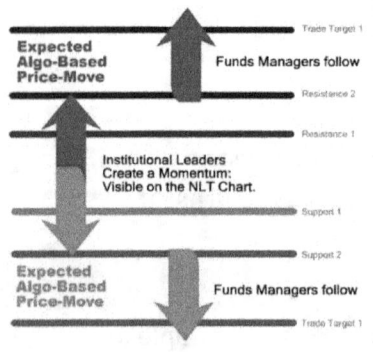

1. **Prices accumulate** prior to a price move and our indicators are identifying this stage by measuring price-, volume- and volatility development, with the NLT-specific market pressure model.
2. Prices **test** the **high/low** of a range prior to breakout. Again, our sensors are triggered and alarm us.
3. Breakout to the next price increment. It shows and is highlighted right on our charts and picked up by our scanners.
4. The **price breakout is noticed** by key market participants and is either:
    – Confirmed – **and we trade it.**
    – **Not confirmed** – and we stay out.

NLT uses dynamic algorithms to predict expected price moves and formulate those targets in Speed Units: SPU

Graph-5: SPU or Speed Unit

NLT **SPU** = Price Move/Time Unit (Price Speed)

A dynamic measure: Constantly Adjusts to the Actual

SPU-Trade-Target:

Minimum expected price move after an institutional engagement is established.

Even so historic performance cannot be taken indicative for future result, this system produces trade setups in excess of the required 66%. When subscribing to a mentorship, you will learn in 20-hours of initial training and a six month mentorship how to execute a business plan for trading that is tailor made to your wants and needs.

Every trader brings a different risk tolerance and affinity to assets and trade environments. Hence, one system does not fit all. This is why NeverLossTrading teaches individual, producing the system and trade focus together with you, helping you to turn yourself into the trader, you want to be.

Trades do only get initiated if the on-the-chart-formulated-minimum-price-threshold is surpassed in the following candle or candles: Depending on the trading method you choose. Buy >

$100.50 means that a trade will only get initiated, when the price of the asset moves at least to $100.51. This method is applicable to Stocks, their Options, Futures and Forex.

Graph-6: Swing Trading Example, Industrial Sector ETF Trade on the NLT Top-Line Chart

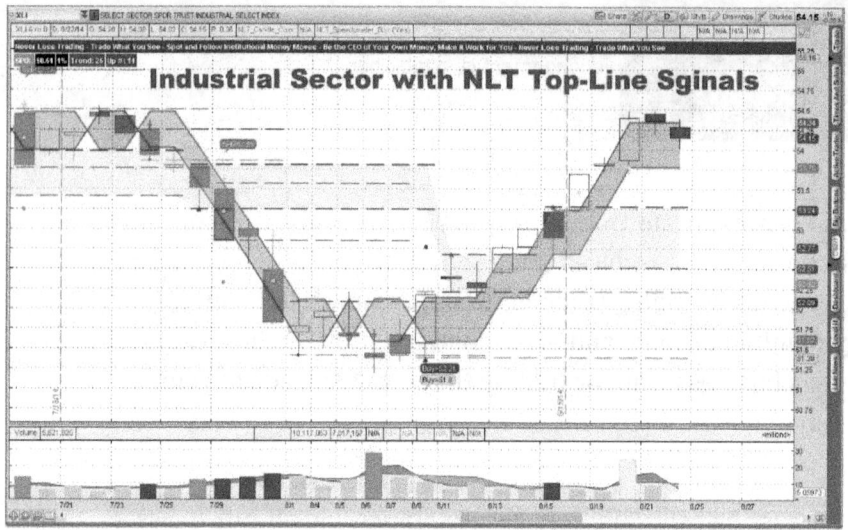

What you see on the chart:

Red covered trade environments favor short selling opportunities. Blue environments indicate strength and prefer long trades.

Institutional engagement is also indicated by colored volume bars and cyan dot highlighted NLT Light Tower Candles.

See the following example for even more details:

Day Trading Example: E-mini S&P 500 Index Futures on the 30 Minute Chart

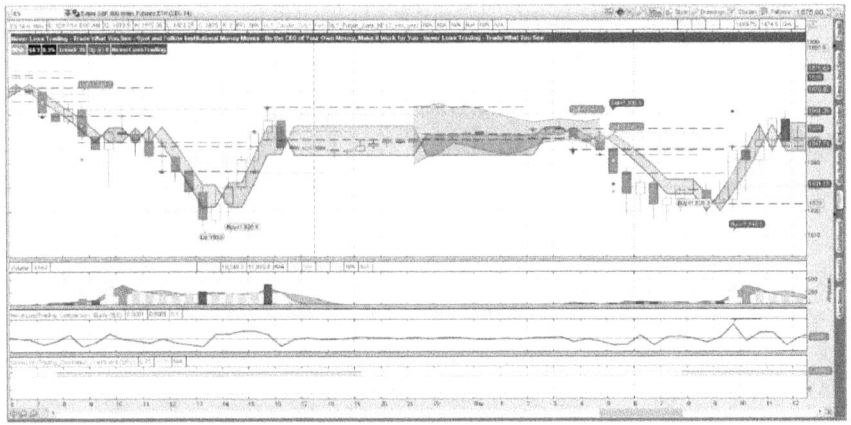

On the chart above, five trades got initiated with four wins (80%) and one loss (second yellow signal, the stop of the trade got reached).

If you want to experience how NeverLossTrading systems work real time, schedule a private consulting hour by: Call 866 455 4520 or mailto:contact@NeverLossTrading.com

Component-2: Stay Engaged

To realize the constant returns, we based our calculation on; you need to stay engaged in the markets, having a way to constantly find trading opportunities for the next trade to come. Key questions are:

Question-1: From the about 40, 000 stocks traded in the US, which ones show an institutional initiated price move.

Quesiton-2: Do all stocks provide favorable trade conditions, given their volume, share of institutional holding, bid/ask spread, holding options or not, their P/E ratio or P/C ration.

Question-3: Which Futures or Forex contracts indicate the desired trade setup and how to trade them best?

New traders at times limit themselves to just trading a couple of assets, but what to do if they do not show a price move, you might miss participating in a chance that might arise in gold or crude oil. In case you do not want to trade futures, but still you want to participate in the price move of a commodity, which instrument to trade: ETF's or Options?

Many questions that you have to answer on your own or you decide to rely on a subscription service or trading-system-inherent-market-scanners, which help you to find those opportunities.

NeverLossTrading Top-Line for example has market scanners build in, where you can constantly scan the markets for opportunities on your preferred time frames and assets: Weeks, days, hours, and minutes.

Helping you to make your life as a trader easier, you can subscribe to NLT Alerts, suited to your individual system in use or trading method:

Core Alerts/Reports:

Day Trading Alerts: Stocks, Options, ETF's, Futures, Forex

Stock Trading Alerts: Stocks for Short-Term Trading, Swing Trading, Long-Term Investments

Long-Term Investor Alerts: Receive a 1-5 week perspective for, Stocks, Options, Futures, Forex

The choices is yours, but in any case, prepare to have a heat seeking finder, telling you which assets have strong individual price moves to pick them and to trade when they move.

When you subscribe to a NLT mentorship, you receive the NLT Alerts, three months for free. However, you can also choose to directly subscribe to NLT Alerts, striving for money making by following favorable trade setups, initiated by institutional money moves: http://neverlosstrading.com/Alerts.html

Example for Favorable Trade Setups Reported by NLT

Primary Signal Symbols	Secondary Signal Symbols	Sentiment	Trade Setup	P/E Ratio	P/C Ratio	Evaluation	NLT Box Trend	Relation to History	Sector	Primary NLT Signal	Secondary NLT Signal
WYNN		Bull	Approved	22	0.73	Bottom Reversal 2	Down	Strong Up	Hotels, Restaurants	Power	
AGO		Bull	Approved	4	0.99	Bottom Reversal 1	Down	Side	Insurance	Power	
MGM		Bull	Approved	76	0.85	Bottom Reversal 1	Down	Side	Hotels, Restaurants	Power	
TWX		Bull	Approved	16	0.13	Bottom Reversal 1	up	Side	Media	Power	
	ADM	Bull	Favorable	17	0.89	Bottom Reversal 1	Down	Side	Food Products		Early up
	MCD	Bull	Favorable	16	1.25	Bottom Reversal 1	Down	Side	Hotels, Restaurants		Swing Point
ICE		Bear	Favorable	60	3.00	Top Weakness	Down	Side	Diversified Financial	Power	
	AA	Bull	Acceptable	179	0.58	Bottom Reversal 1	Up	Side	Metals & Mining		Early up
	APA	Bull	Acceptable	17	0.51	Bottom Reversal 1	Up	Down	Oil, Gas &		Early up
	MDT	Bull	Acceptable	21	0.43	Bottom Reversal 1	Down	Side	Health Care		Swing Point

In the continuation of the report an overall appraisal is given:

Primary Signal Symbols	Secondary Signal Symbols	Last	Daily SPU	Daily SPU to Last %	Move to SPU	Trade Direction	NLT Momentum	NLT Trend	Strongest NLT Indicator	NLT Purple Zone	NLT Volatility	NLT Volume Indicator	Volume (mill.)	Actual Move
WYNN		$ 182.07	$ 7.06	3.9%	109.9%	Up	HF up	down	Power	Change		> Average	4.9	4.5%
AGO		$ 21.70	$ 0.70	3.2%	127.1%	Up	HF up	down	Power		Strong Up	Diff. Up	5.5	4.3%
MGM		$ 21.39	$ 0.91	4.3%	108.8%	Up	HF up	Early up	Power		Strong Up	> Average	0	4.9%
TWX		$ 75.41	$ 2.31	3.1%	138.5%	Up	up	down	Power			high Up	0	4.4%
	ADM	$ 43.17	$ 1.24	2.9%	15.3%	Up	down	Early up	Early up		Strong Up		11.9	0.4%
	MCD	$ 89.91	$ 1.24	1.4%	42.7%	Up	down	down	Swing		wing Poin		1.5	-0.6%
ICE		$ 197.68	$ 4.35	2.2%	119.5%	Down	new	up	Power		trong Dow		5.5	-2.6%
	AA	$ 14.60	$ 0.66	4.5%	15.2%	Up	down	Early up	Early up		wing Poin		3.5	0.7%
	APA	$ 73.23	$ 3.12	4.3%	17.9%	Up	down	Early up	Early up		Strong Up		3.4	0.8%
	MDT	$ 61.81	$ 1.64	2.7%	26.8%	Up	down	down	Swing		wing Poin		0	-0.7%

Finally, leading to define the desired price entry points and the related reward/risk appraisal, ending in proposing maximum prices to pay for NLT preferred options:

Primary Signal Symbols	Secondary Signal Symbols	Last Price	Critical Price Point	Chritical Price Move	Entry Price	Target Price-1	Price Move to Target	Return at Target-1	Stop Approx.	% Risk at 1-SPU	Reward to Risk	Odds Evaluation	Last Hours Price Move	Option Feedback	Exp. Option Price > 30 Days	Exp. Option Price ~20 Days	Exp. Option Price < 14 Days	Weekly Options
WYNN		$ 182.07	$ 184.58	$ 2.65	$ 184.72	$ 189.13	$ 4.41	2.4%	$ 173.03	6.3%	1:2.6	Risky	WYNN	good valu	$ 8.24	$ 5.88	$ 4.94	Yes
AGO		$ 21.70	$ 21.78	$ 0.09	$ 21.79	$ 22.40	$ 0.61	2.8%	$ 20.33	6.7%	1:2.4	Risky		good valu	$ 0.82	$ 0.58	$ 0.49	
MGM		$ 21.39	$ 21.72	$ 0.35	$ 21.74	$ 22.30	$ 0.56	2.6%	$ 20.16	7.3%	1:2.8	Risky	MGM	good valu	$ 1.06	$ 0.76	$ 0.64	Yes
TWX		$ 75.41	$ 76.39	$ 1.03	$ 76.44	$ 77.72	$ 1.28	1.7%	$ 72.42	5.3%	1:3.1	Risky		good valu	$ 2.70	$ 1.93	$ 1.62	Yes
	ADM	$ 43.17	$ 43.47	$ 0.32	$ 43.49	$ 44.71	$ 1.22	2.8%	$ 42.37	2.6%	1:0.9	Favorable		good valu	$ 1.45	$ 1.03	$ 0.87	Yes
	MCD	$ 89.91	$ 90.29	$ 0.40	$ 90.31	$ 91.53	$ 1.22	1.3%	$ 89.34	1.1%	1:0.8	Favorable		good valu	$ 1.45	$ 1.03	$ 0.87	Yes
ICE		$ 197.68	$ 197.25	$ (0.52)	$ 197.16	$ 193.33	$ 3.83	1.9%	$ 202.80	2.9%	1:1.4	Favorable		good valu	$ 5.08	$ 3.63	$ 3.05	-
	AA	$ 14.60	$ 14.65	$ 0.06	$ 14.66	$ 15.31	$ 0.65	4.4%	$ 14.01	4.5%	1:1	Acceptable		good valu	$ 0.77	$ 0.55	$ 0.46	Yes
	APA	$ 73.23	$ 74.53	$ 1.36	$ 74.59	$ 77.65	$ 3.06	4.1%	$ 70.66	5.3%	1:1.2	Acceptable		good valu	$ 3.64	$ 2.60	$ 2.18	Yes
	MDT	$ 61.81	$ 62.84	$ 1.06	$ 62.87	$ 64.48	$ 1.61	2.6%	$ 61.28	2.5%	1:0.9	Acceptable		good valu	$ 1.91	$ 1.37	$ 1.15	Yes

Imagine the time this will save you and the accuracy your trading will get from a detailed trade setup alert like this or take any other comparable offer on the market, but stay engaged.

Component-3: Feedback

Who likes administration?

However, for you to turn yourself into the trader, you want to be, you need to seek out for feedback. Again, you can try to replicate on your own how well you did on specific trades or you decide to take the advice from a coach, who is familiar with your trading system and can gives you the final hints to get you over the hump.

Thus:

Document your trades, best with a screen shot from the trade setup you found on the screen and do the same, when the trade is concluded, either in a win or loss.

With the help of this document, check you initial assumptions in respect to:

Entry: Did you pick a trade situation which was according to the rules of your system?

Exit: Did you stay in the trade until it concluded at the specifically set target?

Stop: Did you work with the stop level, you decided that is needed for giving the asset price the wiggle room to develop in the desired direction without getting stopped.

Unfortunately many new traders constantly violate Entry and Stop rules. Why is that? The fear of losing in a trade leads the new trader to take an early exit, either by taking profits early, or by trailing stops too tight. Both cases are very detrimental on the potential trading results, leading to a chain of: Small gain, small gain, bigger loss.

If you wanted to learn golf to make money, do you think working on your swing on your own would get you to where you wanted to be? Hence, find a coach, who gives you constant feedback on your trades, until you get them right on Entries, Exits, and Stops.

NeverLossTrading offers such service by a six months mentorship, where you can send in all trades as screen-shots and you get either written or verbal feedback.

Graph-7: Student Example

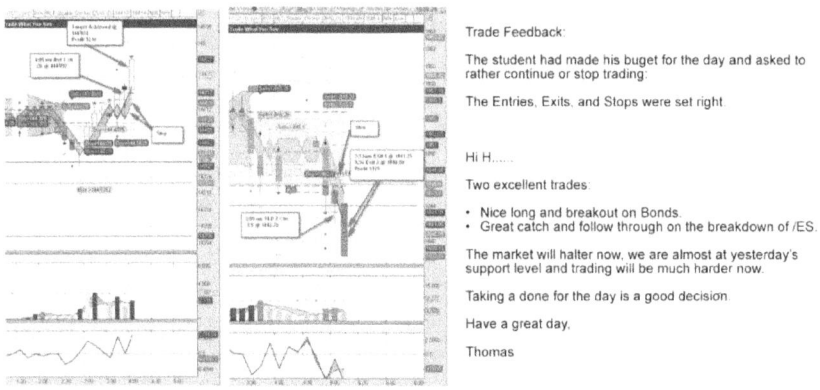

Component-4: Risk Management

In trading, we predict a probable outcome, but we control how much risk we take per trade.

Hence, you either have to work with an education institution or on your own to clearly define risk rules and act open them.

In the student example, you saw a positive "done for the day" exit; however, you also need to agree with yourself a maximum number of losses or a maximum dollar loss that brings you back to the drawing board to re-iterate why things did not work in your favor.

In addition, your trading is better on when you find an agreement of how you adjust lot sizes in accordance to the odds ratio of each trade setup:

Odds Ratio: (Probability of success * Reward) / (Probability of Losing*Risk)

This factor should be above 1.5 for you to even start trading. In addition, you are much better on adjusting your lot-size by the referring odds ratio. Please check the example below which compares a stock and option trade at the same trade setup:

Odds Ratio and Position Sizing

Risky Trades: 1/2-Lot or not Trade; Usual Setups: 1-Lot; Favorable Setups: 2-Lots; Home Run Setups: 4-Lots.

Stock Trade Evaluation

Stock Symbol		BBD	Input
Trade Direction		up	Select
NeverLossTrading Signal		Dark Green	Select
1-SPU Measure	$	0.51	Input
Entry Price	$	14.97	Input
Target-1 (no hindrance)	$	15.47	Input
Stop Price	$	14.58	Input
Price Move to Target	$	0.50	Calculated
Price Move to Stop	$	0.39	Calculated
Risk/Unit		2.6%	Calculated
Reward/Unit		3.3%	Calculated
Reward/Risk		1.2:1	Calculated

Stock Trade Evaluation Results

Odds Evaluation	Cleared Risk Managment
SPU Evaluation	Check Your Stop Placement: Seems Tight
Odds Ratio	2.4:1
Potential Lot Size	2-Lots on sound retrun on captial

Lot Equation

Account Size	$	50,000	Input
Assumed Active Positions to Hold		10	Input
Average Lot Size (calculated):	$	5,000	Calculated
2-Lots on sound retrun on captial of		668	Shares
Investment Amount:	$	10,000	Calculated
Trade Reward at 668 Shares	$	334	3.3%
Trade Risk at 668 Shares	$	261	2.6%

Option Trade Evaluation

Stock Symbol		BBD	Auto Selected from Stock Setup
Put or Call Option		Call	Auto Selected from Stock Setup
Time to Expiration (days)		26	Input
Delta (enter positive values)		0.30	Input
Price for the Option	$	0.23	Input
Bid/Ask Spread	$	0.02	Input
Critical Price Point	$	14.58	Calculated
Option Price at Target	$	0.36	Calculated
Estimated Reward/Contract		57%	Calculated
Approximated Risk/Contract		75%	Calculated
Reward/Risk Ratio		0.7:1	Calculated

Option Trade Evaluation Results

Option Price Evaluation	Acceptable
Time Evaluation	Enough Time
Odds Ratio	1.4:1
Potential Lot Size	max 1/2-Lot

Lot Equation

Dedicated Option Budget	$	10,000	Input
Assumed Active Positions to Hold		10	Input
Average Lot Size	$	1,000	Calculated
max 1/2-Lot of BBD equates to:		21.73	Contracts
Investment Amount	$	500	Calculated
Trade Reward at 21.73 Contracts	$	282	56.5%
Trade Risk at 21.73 Contracts	$	376	75.2%

The example of the BBD-share shows that the stock trade has a more favorable trade setup than the option trade; thus, potentially investing into 2-lots on the stock trade and maximum 1/2-Lot in the option trade (if you even accept the option trade), results from the calculation scheme.

We hope, the effort we put into the presentation and this article helps you as a trader to move along for your better.

If you like to learn more about NeverLossTrading, take the chance and test us live. Schedule a free consulting hour, where we get together online with you, share our screens and answer your questions:

mailto:contact@NeverLossTrading.com

Call: +1 866 455 4520

In case you are not yet subscribed to our free trading tips and market reports, sign up here:

http://www.neverlosstrading.com/Reports/FreeReports.html

Good trading,

Thomas Barrman
contact@NeverLossTrading.com
NeverLossTrading
www.NeverLossTrading.com

Disclaimer

This publication is designed to provide accurate and authoritative information in regard to the subject matter covered. It is sold with the understanding that the publisher is not engaged in rendering legal, financial advice, accounting, or other professional service. If legal advice or other expert assistance is required, the services of a competent professional person should be sought.

Following the rules of the SEC (Security Exchange Commission), we advise all readers that it should not be assumed that present or future performance of applying NeverLossTrading (a division of Nobel Living, LLC) would be profitable or equal the performance of our examples. The reader should recognize that the risk of trading securities, stocks, options, futures can be substantial. Customers must consider all relevant risk factors, including their own personal financial situation before trading. In our teaching of NeverLossTrading, in our books, newsletters, webinars and our involvement in the Investment Clubs, neither NOBEL Living, LLC, the parent company of NeverLossTrading, nor any of the speakers, staff or members act as stockbrokers, broker dealers, or registered investment advisers. We worked out trading concepts we use on a daily basis and share them through education with our readers, members and clients.

Chapter 7 - Finding the Perfect Trade Setup By David Choe

Traders are always searching for the holy grail in trading, but to really make money in the markets is to be able to find the perfect trade setup at the right time. That's where CandlestickFigures.com comes in. This is a proprietary software which allows traders to custom design and create any candlestick setup to search for in any market, any timeframe and any asset class. This is a simple to use product that will save you hours of time in research. This is completely different from your candlestick scanners that come with your trading platforms or anything else on the market due to the customization ability.

This is to be used in the NinjaTrader platform. The reason NinjaTrader was used is due to the amazing technical ability of the platform. Also an important factor is that you can download it for FREE. There is a simple two step setup to import the software into the platform for easy use. Once installed you can begin setting up some pretty complicated scans and searching for the right setup to trade.

To use the software we have encoded all of the technical aspects to allow a very user friendly tool to use for even the most inexperienced computer users. Setting up the scanner is simple. First, you open the market analyzer in NinjaTrader. You have the option to set up any timeframe from minutes, hours, days, weeks etc. This makes it ideal for the day trader, swing trader and position trader. Then you select the CandlestickFigures indicator to open up all the parameters. From there you can setup any candlestick setup up to 5 candlesticks. You have the ability to set these candlesticks in any configuration using a set of predefined conditions. This allows an infinite set of possible combinations for you to try.

The drop down list of candlesticks includes all of the basic individual candlesticks available. They include the hammer, inverted hammer, small green candle, small red candle, doji, bullish candle and bearish candle. We have made the definitions of these candlesticks slightly broader to include more results into the scans. By making the definitions too restrictive in terms of coding, that would eliminate many results. For instance, a doji usually closes at the open, but we have made the definition to include any close near the open. This will include the spinning tops as well. If we made the definition to only include at the close, then the scanner would not include any doji candle whose close was a penny off. Also the hammer and inverted hammer candles are included with any close near the open. The small green and red candles are defined as any candle whose whole body size from high to low is at least twice the size of the body size of the candle. Finally, the bullish and bearish candlesticks are a broad definition as well. The bullish candlestick is defined as any positive candlestick whose close is at least 50 percent of the whole body size of the candle. The bearish candlestick is the reverse of this. It is defined as any negative candlestick whose close is at least 50 percent or below the whole candle size. Then the user simply picks any of these candlesticks in order to begin creating the candlestick setup desired.

Next the user has the ability to select conditions to describe where to place these candlesticks. This allows the user to create any configuration desired to scan for the most sophisticated patterns. Again with a simple drop down menu, the user can select any position. The conditions always refer to the current candlestick in relation to a previous candlestick. The first condition is "greater than previous high." This describes your current candlestick to break the high of any previous candlestick in the pattern. The second condition is "less than previous low." This describes your current candlestick to break the low of any previous candlestick. The third condition is "whole candle inside previous candle." This includes any current candlestick whose high and low are inside the high and low of any previous candlestick. The fourth condition is "same high and low of previous candle." This places the current candlestick next to a previous candlestick with the exact same high and low. The fifth condition includes "whole candle engulfs previous candle." This describes a condition where the current candlesticks high is greater than a previous candles high, and the current candlesticks low is lower than the previous candles low. The sixth condition is "low greater than or equal to 50 percent wick low." This is a unique condition where the previous candlestick must have a lower wick such as a hammer candle. The midpoint of the lower wick is calculated and measured. If the current candlestick cannot break the midpoint of the lower wick and instead breaks upward, it is a valid result. This sometimes leads to short term reversals to the upside. The last condition is the reverse of this. It is "high is less than or equal to 50 percent wick high." This looks back at a previous candlestick with an upper wick such as an inverted hammer. If the current candlestick cannot break above the 50 percent midpoint of the upper wick and instead breaks downward then it may lead to a short term reversal to the downside.

You also have the ability to describe any condition in relation to any previous candlestick. The conditions do not necessarily have to be in relation to the candlestick directly next to the current one. This allows for so many more combinations and patterns to be formed. For instance, when configuring the fourth candlestick, the user has the option to place a bullish candle to break the high of the previous candlestick 1, 2, or 3.

Finally, there are some great filter options for the scanner. The user can select to have positive results displayed with any text desired. Also, the user can select to filter out any negative results to only display the positive ones. This comes in handy when scanning large indexes such as the S & P 500.

Once scanning results are displayed, the user can input the results in a chart to evaluate and see if it is the perfect setup. The results can be displayed to show on each tick or on the close of the candlestick bar. In day trading I prefer to use the calculate on each tick to give results. That way I can evaluate the trade within the current timeframe to see if it fits my criteria along with other technical indicators before pulling the trigger on a trade.

Here is one example of a unique setup found using the scanner. The first candlestick in the pattern is the inverted hammer. The second candlestick is a normal hammer that breaks the low of the

1st inverted hammer. Then the third candlestick is a bullish candlestick which breaks the 2nd hammer candle. Another variation of this is to have the bullish candlestick break above the 1st inverted hammer candle as well. To understand the logic behind this, one needs to look behind the actual candlesticks to see the buyers and sellers. After the 1st candlestick, many traders will look to short a breakdown below the low of the inverted hammer, but when the next candle forms a quick hammer reversal it worries the traders who are short. Once the 3rd candlestick breaks above the 2nd candlestick, then many traders realize they are wrong and begin to cover their shorts. That is what leads to a short term reversal to the upside. This is a candlestick setup which doesn't have a traditional name for it. That's why it is impossible to find anywhere else. That's the value in this software to be able to create any candlestick setup imaginable. All of the traditional patterns can be scanned for as well.   This will simplify your research and save you hours of time searching through stock charts. Hope it helps with your trading and I hope you create your own "candlestick figures" today.

David Choe
choesen@hotmail.com
Choesen Trade LLC
CandlestickFigures.com

Chapter 8- The EminiScalp ABL AutoTrade Strategy by Al McWhirr

Trading is easy.

The click of the mouse is all it takes to enter a trade. That is easy enough. But please, don't let the first sentence of this article fool you. Successful trading, now that is not so easy. In fact, it is almost impossible for the majority of traders.

Successful trading may not mean the same thing to all traders. If a trader is able to squeak out a minimal amount of profit daily or weekly, he or she may declare themselves a successful trader. There may be those traders who believe success depends upon them meeting or exceeding a minimum and certain profit level daily or weekly. And of course, some traders feel that if they break even or have a minimal loss at the end of the day, they have met success. The reasoning here may be that they will persevere and steadier profits will come.

Since the very large majority of traders are not successful for one reason or another, it is the perseverance that keeps most earnest traders motivated and working towards success. The statistics seem to indicate that those who choose to enter the business have a very minimal chance of surviving. Although success may seem to be elusive, some do succeed. With the onslaught of webinars and trading rooms, it looks as though most traders are looking for a method or a trader who is successful.

But, like any successful business, trading requires focus, effort and lots of hard WORK. THERE ARE NO SHORTCUTS.

Some traders believe trading success comes easy and that they should be able to do it in a very short time. Once they believe they have trading mastered, they may to begin trade live. Being in a rush and not taking the time to learn has its consequences.

Here's the scenario…One bad trade and you become anxious. The next bad trade and you become agitated. The third bad trade you are outright aggravated. You start to doubt yourself and your method. You take some time and SIM trade and over a short period of time, you gain your composure and confidence and feel that you will recover. At this point trading becomes about recovery, not profit. No doubt this works on your emotions.

If a trader contacts a vendor and purchases a method, it is up to the purchaser to follow the rules, as per the documentation that accompanies the method. There is a reason for this. The basic reason is discipline. If a trader adds their own elements to the method, such as trend lines, Bollinger bands or the like, this makes the purchased method valueless. The discipline is to follow the directions exactly.

Not all trades are going to be profitable. Stops are part of the business. The goal is to manage the stops with the successful trades so that profits can be realized.

My discipline is to trade what I see on my charts. Many traders, for some reason, believe that following and trading the news is the way to go. The content of news in no way influences my trading.

Has gold bottomed out, is the CL about to back off, is the ES overbought or oversold. Will an impending storm in the Gulf affect oil prices? This type of news is not important to me. Of course, news is important and does make the market move. But in reality, is the normal day trader going to be part of the initial move? It would be foolish for the trader who has limited experience, as well as a limited trading account, to attempt to trade the news. The results can be disastrous.

It doesn't matter what the content of the news is, what matters is what the news does. Traders are unable to control news, so to attempt to trade it can be devastating. Of course, news does influence price, and this influence in turn creates the critical trade areas that we determine as our trade areas.

With our EminiScalp ABL AutoTrade, there are specific critical trade areas that can be traded during the news events. A short discussion of our EminiScalp ABL AutoTrade Strategy will be discussed later in this article and in more detail in our TradersWorld Webinar as well as on our website at www.eminiscalp.com.

If one observes what takes place when a news item hits the market, and generally we all know when this will happen, the price will normally react. Who or what is making the price move the way it does? It could be investment house traders, bank traders, or other large entities. I personally do not believe it is the normal day trader. Does it really matter who is making the market move? For those who believe the market is random or not predictive, I beg to differ.

As I had mentioned previously, we generally know when news will occur. There is no hard and fast rule that requires anyone or any entity to trade this news, but since price commonly moves one way or the other, then it stands to reason someone or something is making this happen. We, as traders, can count on the fact that price will move. But, is it wise to trade this news? I don't think so. A trader may know where the price may want to go but it may whip around before it ever gets there. There is no reason to be part of that chaos. I suggest that a trader be patient because the price movement during this time will create some critical trade areas and this is what day trading is all about. In my estimation, there are about five critical trade areas created during the trading day.

If one was to look at his or her chart, I am sure that a few of these areas would be visible. I define a critical trade area as an area where price was at one time, and may want to return to sometime in the immediate future. As an example, watch for a news item that comes out at 10 AM east. Observe what the price does. It may drop dramatically or move up with the same gusto. Then what happens? Price will attempt to return from where it started. Where price moves during this time period may produce trade areas that we should be interested in, as these could be deemed critical trade areas that may be meaningful throughout the trading day.

Too many traders are focused on their indicators and not on the price. Price is what is important and where the price moves is significant. Take a chart and remove the indicators and just watch the price. See where it goes. Does it really matter why it goes where it does? Absolutely not. It just matters that it moves there. You should be trading the chart, not the news.

If you study your chart(s) over a period of time, you may be able to identify these trade areas. If so, great, as you are now noticing something that probably was allusive in the past. Knowing where price may go is only part of the equation. Knowing where to enter is very critical. You may have your eye on a great trade area and really believe that price will reach it sometime during the trading session. Would it be wise to just jump in with an entry? I don't think so, not without knowing what is happening between your entry and possible target area. If your trade area means that you must take a long trade, you still need to be cautious. Even though the market may be moving up, price will normally move up, possibly reverse for a time since some traders may be exiting their trades, then move up once again on more buying activity. Unless you have deep pockets and can withstand price moving against you for a time, it is imperative that your entry has a high probability of giving you profit. You don't always have to exit at the exact target price; it may be prudent to take profits before the price reaches your target. Actually, it may be beneficial to take profits at a certain level with one or two contracts and let another contract or two run with a trailing stop.

When in a trade, your emotions may get the best of you if you see profit then the price backs off. You may bail out with a loss or a break even trade. After you exit, you watch price move to your target. It is very difficult for many traders to watch price reverse on them, believing the market is taking a turn against their position, when it just may be other traders exiting their positions for some profit. The market usually will never go straight up or down. There are rest stops. So, where are the profitable entry areas and how do we determine them? For most traders, knowing where to enter is very difficult. It is also difficult, if not downright impossible, for some traders to actually take a real money trade. This is not uncommon in this business. So, what can be done? Other than to spend a great deal of time SIM trading your successful method, you may want to consider an auto trade method.

A trader should know entries and exits because that is what successful trading is all about. But, determining these areas may be difficult for many traders.

In order to make this a bit easier and hopefully less stressful, I have developed my EminiScalp ABL AutoTrade Strategy. As I had mentioned earlier, knowing critical trade areas is key to successful trades. The EminiScalp ABL AutoTrade Strategy is designed to assist the trader with possible entries when price reaches the current high or low. Many times a trader will watch price move up and assume that price can't go any higher. They may take a short just because they feel that the move is exhausted. To their dismay, price continues to rise and the trader gets stopped. This same scenario can also happen when price moves to the low of the day. Our ABL strategy is designed to assess a variety of trading factors when price reaches certain specific trade areas. When conditions permit, a trade signal will appear. If enabled for autotrade, the trader is automatically entered into the trade. Each trader should be familiar with the NinjaTrader Super DOM, as individual profit management is determined by each trader. I discuss this further in the TradersWorld webinar. A trader has the option of turning the autotrade off. When this happens, the signals will still appear, but there will be no auto trade entries. The trader has the option of taking these signals manually if he or she so desires.

I have included a few screen shots illustrating the entry areas.

Below is a shot of the YM at the open. The great feature about the ABL is that it is possible to trade the open as well as any news events. As can be seen on the screen shot, the price continues lower and lower. Most traders may think that after a 3rd or 4th new low, a long may be possible. On this particular chart, the ABL correctly determines the long entry.

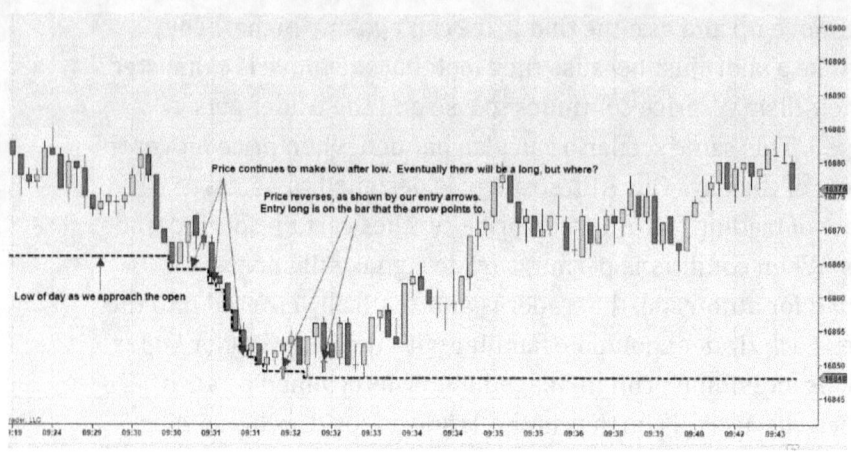

The screen shot below is of the CL. Four nice entries within about a ½ hour period.

The EminiScalp ABL AutoTrade Strategy can be used with just about all markets.

Our EminiScalp ABL AutoTrade Strategy is already preset, there are no adjustments to me made once installed. Just set your session times as well as any time(s) that you don't want to trade, and you are ready to go.

The screen shots below show the NEWS times where a trader has the ability to turn off the auto entries at specific times.

Alerts	
BuyAlert	Alert1.wav
SellAlert	Alert2.wav
UseAudioAlerts	False
News	
News1Start	09:55:00
News1Stop	10:05:00
News2Start	-00:00:01
News2Stop	-00:00:01
News3Start	-00:00:01
News3Stop	-00:00:01
News4Start	-00:00:01
News4Stop	-00:00:01
News5Start	-00:00:01
News5Stop	-00:00:01
News6Start	-00:00:01
News6Stop	-00:00:01
NewsEnabled1	False
NewsEnabled2	False
NewsEnabled3	False
NewsEnabled4	False
NewsEnabled5	False
NewsEnabled6	False
Parameters	

If you are an early riser or a night owl, you can set the session time to suit your trading schedule.

More information regarding our EminiScalp ABL Autotrade Strategy will be available on our TradersWorld Webinar as well as on our website at www.eminiscalp.com. If you have any questions, please contact me at info@eminiscalp.com.

Chapter 9 - Simple and Practical Tips to Easily and Dramatically Improve Your Trading Psychology By Dr. Barry Burns

What Moves the Markets?

Do Fundamentals matter? Yes, but the information received is often late, can be revised, and may not even be accurate when released. It can also be hard to correlate with the movement of the market you're trading as we see that sometimes markets go up on bad news and down on good news!

So what really moves the markets if it's not a company's fundamentals or news?

Markets move on the actions people take based on their BELIEFS and FEELINGS about the market.

Of course being a massive auction house, no one person's actions move the market. The markets move as the result of LOTS of people – and therefore the markets move according to the principles of Mass Psychology.

This has led me to trade the markets using technical analysis rather than fundamental analysis.

Technical Analysis is the Math of Mass Psychology.

The "Nature" of the Markets

The movement of the market is the movement of mass psychology. So the "nature" of the market is HUMAN NATURE.

1. Charts are maps of collective human BEHAVIOR.

2. The market isn't LIKE people, it IS people.

3. Nothing gets plotted on a chart until people take ACTION.

4. Charts don't map people's thoughts, beliefs, hopes and fears ... they map COMMITMENTS!

The Nature of People

If the nature of the markets is the nature of people, it behooves us to ask about the nature of people. Here are five aspects of human nature and how those aspects are reflected in charts:

1. Goal Oriented – Trends

2. "3 Steps Forward, 2 Steps Back" – Oscillations

3. "Getting Stuck" – Consolidation

4. Work and Rest – Cycles

5. "All Nighters" and Vacation – Expanding and Contracting Cycles

6. Emotional Beings: Love and Hate, Overreact and passive aggressive – Market Bubbles A Practical Exercise to Help You Think Different than the Masses:

It's no secret that most traders lose money. Trading is extremely risky and most people who attempt to make money in the markets end up losers. One of the keys to success, therefore, is to think different than the masses. You must be better than the "losers" (I don't use that term in a derogatory way, but simply in a literal way referring to those who consistently lose money).

Here's an exercise I engaged in for six months that helped me become familiar with how the losing traders are thinking and acting. I used this information to think and act differently than them. I invite you to do the same.

Attend several free live trading chat rooms where amateur traders are actively communicating with each other and watch the charts in conjunction with their comments.

Remember, the masses are wrong most of the time. So what you're hearing is the inner dialog and the behavior of the losers.

Do this for 3-6 months (listening to their comments and watching the charts in conjunction with their comments), and before long the sheer repetition of their same comments to the same price patterns will become engrained in your brain cells. You'll be able to hear their voices in your mind. Eventually you'll be able to do the reverse:

Without even being in the chat room, you'll be able to watch the charts, and in your mind hear the dialog of the losers!

The result is that you'll know what the losing traders are doing during certain price patterns (they're very consistent in doing the exact wrong things) and you can avoid making those mistakes yourself (and perhaps even take the opposite side of their trade).

In "Market Wizards," (Publisher: Wiley) Jack Schwager interviews some of the world's most successful traders in search of a commonality that can lead to success for others. His conclusion after the interviews:

"What set these traders apart? Most people think that winning in the markets has something to do with finding the secret formula. The truth is that any common denominator among the traders I interviewed had more to do with ATTITUDE than APPROACH."

In his follow-up book, "The New Market Wizards," (Publisher: HarperBusiness) Jack Schwager wrote:

"'We has met the enemy, and it is us.' The famous quote from Walt Kelly's cartoon strip, "Pogo," would provide as fitting a one-line summation of the art of trading as any. Time and time again, those whom I interviewed for this book and its predecessor stressed the absolutely critical role of psychological elements in trading success. When asked what was important to success, the Market Wizards never talked about indicators or techniques, but rather about such things as discipline, emotional control, patience, and mental attitude toward losing. The message is clear: The key to winning in the markets is internal, not external."

It's obvious that to be a successful trader, you need a viable trading method with setups, rules and a plan that works. Without that, no amount of "psychology" is going to help you.

Try Before You Buy

Unfortunately there are many traders who have a viable trading method, who never know it, because they have never tested the method divorced from their emotions.

For this reason I highly recommend paper trading any new method you're trying (even if you're a seasoned trader) for at least 3-6 months before you put a single real-money trade on the line. This paper trading must be done in real-time, not after the fact, so rather than literally using paper, I recommend you use a trading simulator or demo account to test drive your trading method.

This gives the additional benefit of helping you learn the timing of the entries. Learning to enter your orders without hesitation is a critical trading behavior for your success. It will also help you learn whether the methodology fits your personality.

By paper trading for 3-6 months, and keeping track of every trade (using trading logs), you'll find that the method works ... as long as you trade it without emotion.

Before you can trade successfully, you need to have confidence in your method. Without confidence in your method, you will second-guess the rules, get discouraged during draw downs, and fearfully stay out of good setups. The ONLY thing that will create that confidence is success. And the best way to achieve a winning track record is to trade without emotion ... and at the beginning, that means trading without money.

After successfully paper trading for an extended amount of time, it's time to start trading with a SMALL AMOUNT of real money. Now if you start losing, then you know the variable is the emotion of trading with money.

Once we solve the problem of finding a successful trading method, then we have to deal with the problem of YOU!

Overtrading is one of the biggest challenges to new traders. But one of the hallmarks of successful traders is that they actually trade very little. They wait for the PERFECT setups because they know that's the

ONLY time that the odds are really with them, and that makes the difference between trading and gambling.

Even in the gambling world, however, the professionals know this. Profitable poker players fold on more hands than they play. If they don't have a strong opening hand with a high probability of winning, they simply fold and wait for a better one.

In his book, "Money Management for Gamblers (Publisher: Lyle Stuart), John Patrick writes:

"People who are way better educated than me rip my theories from here to Hades and back. They claim gambling is all math and statistical analysis. They will never grasp the true meaning of gambling – because they have never been there.

... People who think that a math equation is gonna give them a leg up on winning ought have that leg whack them in the area where they sit on their brains. ... you absolutely must have money management ... Topped off with a healthy dose of discipline."

... [The pros] don't make MISTAKES, and they don't have tells. Patience is a virtue, stupidity is a one-way street to disaster, talk is minimal, and mercy is absent. Make a MISTAKE and seven vultures circle the wagons, waiting to divide the spoils. When the night is done and you are fortunate enough to escape with a small profit, the ride home gives you only a short time to count your blessings and your money."

If you're trading every day of the week and you're not trading well with a successful methodology, it's most likely because you're making mistakes.

So is there a way to eliminate mistakes? No one ever becomes a perfect trader, but the first step to reducing your mistakes is to identify them.

Here are 10 Commandments which are general rules. We'll translate them into specific "mistakes" as they would relate to the rules of our trading methodology.

1. Don't Chase a Move.

2. Don't Trade Choppy Markets.

3. Don't Fight the Trend.

4. Don't Trade Too Many Contracts for Your Account Size.

5. Don't Trade for the "Action."

6. Do Guard Your Capital; it's Your Lifeblood.

7. Don't Try to Recover Losses with Emotional "Revenge Trading."

8. Don't Trade the Market, Only Trade Your Rules.

9. Don't Place Your Stops Too Close.

10. Don't Take Profits Too Soon.

One of my favorite sayings in trading is:

"Successful Trading is Simply a Matter of NOT MAKING MISTAKES."

I have found this to be a great truism in my trading life. As long as I don't make mistakes, I come out ahead at the end of the week or month. Of course that is predicated on the issue of first having a viable trading methodology.

The "mistakes" I refer to are the 10 Commandments listed above. This is my list which reflects the most common mistakes I found myself making. I compiled this list from other traders and my own experience.

I encourage you to add or subtract to it. Make it your own. Use this as a springboard for creating your own list that aligns with your own unique trading struggles.

Your goal is to trade your method as strictly as possible and without making any of these mistakes.

Avoiding mistakes is a matter of self-discipline.

Although I can't give you self-discipline, I will give you an exercise that can help you tremendously with the issue. You still have to actually stick to it, but if nothing else it can serve as a mirror to reflect back to you how out of control your trading may actually be. The exercise is simple. Keep a trading log of every trade you take. Rather than simply recording your entry and exit prices and times, also record any mistakes you made on each trade (refer to the "10 Commandments" above for a list of mistakes).

At the end of each day, transfer the results of your trading day, including your mistakes, to a weekly trading log where you record the summary of your trading day on one row.

Over time, you'll notice patterns of mistakes you make consistently that you're not currently consciously aware of.

Finally, subtract all the losses of trades in which you made mistakes, and see what you're trading income would be without those trades. In many cases, people find that they'd be successful traders right now if they simply eliminated their mistakes!

Here are sample copies of my trading logs. You're welcome to use these or create your own: Dr. Barry Burns is the owner of Top Dog Trading, the author of "Trend Trading for Dummies,"

DAILY TRADING LOG	DATE: / /					TIMES OF ECONOMIC REPORTS:			
Successful Trading is Simply a Business of NOT MAKING MISTAKES. That's what separates the pro who makes money from the educated amateur.						1. _____ 3. _____			
						2. _____ 4. _____			
ENTRY TIME	TRADING VEHICLE	LONG/SHORT ENTRY PRICE	PROTECTIVE STOP	1ST TARGET	2ND TARGET	EXIT TIME	EXIT PRICE	$ GAIN/LOSS	TOTAL GAIN/LOSS
NOTES:						MISTAKES:			
NOTES:						MISTAKES			
NOTES:						MISTAKES			

DATE	WIN/LOSS	TOTAL P/L	AVERAGE $ WIN/$LOSS	COM-MISS	NET P/L; % ACCT	# OF MIS-TAKES	NET P/L w/o MIS-TAKES	MISTAKES
WEEK TOTALS								

TRADE LOG FOR THE WEEK OF _____ to _____

Dr. Barry Burns is the owner of Top Dog Trading, the author of "Trend Trading for Dummies," has presented seminars for the Chicago Mercantile Exchange, the Eurex Exchange, MetaStock and trading expos around the country.

Barry Burns
mmentors@hotmail.com
Top Dog Trading
www.topdogtrading.com

Chapter 10- Why do traders love Nadex Binary Options? By Gail Mercer

"Why do traders love Nadex Binary Options?" The reason is simple. Most pitfalls that cause a trader to fail are avoided with Binary Options, thus insuring the trader a greater chance of success. Most traders fail for one or more of the following reasons:

1. They are undercapitalized. What does this mean? Most traders, especially with the downturn of the economy in the last few years, only have $5,000-15,000 to start their accounts. They need to make enough money to support themselves and their families. Each week is going to present at least two to three days of sideways movement. Sideways movement will cause them to lose money in the form of losing trades. If a trader starts with $5,000, and has five consecutive losing days, he could be down 30% in his account (or $1,500) if risking only $100 per trade, three trades per day.

2. This leads to the fear of losing more money. Most traders understand that they need to increase their risk to reward per trade to overcome losses, but they have a limited supply of capital. A trader will then begin to question every entry. Typically because of the fear they are experiencing, a trader will not take the first, second or even third setup. After seeing the market

move in his direction and calculating how much he "would have" made, the trader may finally choose to enter a trade only to be stopped out yet again.

3. At this point, the trader decides to find new indicators and a new methodology. After all, "it can't be me", the trader tells himself. The trader will then follow a new methodology and lose more money. A trader may even pull money out of his savings account and justify the action by saying it was the first set of indicators that lost the money.

4. Usually one of two things will happen next. The trader may decide that it is the stops that are causing his losses. He may decide that they are too tight, so he will enlarge them -- resulting in even bigger losses. Or, the trader will simply sit and stare at the screen, never able to pull the trigger. He feels like a loser. He wants to make this work so badly, but simply cannot pull the trigger. Words cannot describe the depth of despair he feels. He questions his ability to trade and wonders how he could be that stupid. The trader's emotional anguish may be extreme.

5. Usually, by this point, the trader decides to take a break from trading. He will need to find a job, but will still watch the markets. The trader has been "bitten" by the trading bug and nothing compares to trading. The trader remembers the highs of making money quickly in the market and it is hard to get excited about any other type of work.

6. The trader saves up money again, and comes back to the markets determined to make it work this time. He has increased his knowledge of the markets and of price action, and is convinced that this time it will be different. The first couple of trades are awesome. He doubles his account. "Oh, yeah, he knows what he is doing this time!" Then the market hits and hits hard. He loses a couple of trades and he is angry. He is not going to let the market take his hard earned money again. What happens next? The markets take all the gains and then some. Again, desperation returns.

Typically this cycle repeats itself over and over again. Breaking the cycle is one of the hardest obstacles in a trader's path.

Now, let's look at the differences with Nadex:

1. There are no margin calls. The risk is paid up front (the strike price). This means that a trader cannot move his stop farther away from price or have the markets jump over his stop (which happens frequently during market volatility).

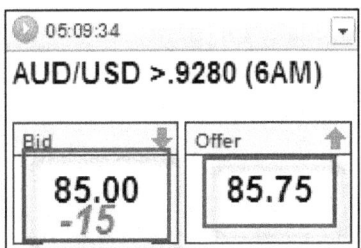

2. Losses are capped going into the trade. This means that when the trader enters the trade, his total potential loss is paid up front. Because the loss is paid up front, the trader has more control and realizes what he can lose before ever placing the trade. For example, in the AUD/USD image, the maximum loss on the offer side is $85.75 and the maximum risk on the bid side is $15.00 ($100 - $85). If a trader buys the Binary Option for the AUDUSD, $85.75 is immediately deducted from his account.

3. In this example, the Nadex Binary Options are worth $100 at expiration of the contract, and the profit potential is only $14.25. If the trader opted to sell the binary option, $15 would be deducted from his account. In this example, the options would be worth $0 at expiration and the profit potential would be $85. However, the probabilities are greater on the "buy" side and are less on the "sell" side. (This will be addressed in another article.)

4. Profits are also capped. The order entry on every Nadex Binary Option shows the maximum loss and profit on every trade. This encourages the trader to think his trade through. For example, "the risk on the trade is $23.50 and the potential reward is a maximum of $76.50 or a 1:3 risk to reward ratio." Instead of dreaming about the hundreds of dollars he can make on the trade, the maximum profit on each side is known upfront. Because this is shown upfront, it encourages the trader to "think through" the process of the trade before entering the market. This is a realistic approach. This is intraday trading, and day traders typically do not take thousands of dollars in profit at a time. Instead, day traders take small profits throughout the day. Look at a successful

trader's equity graph and chances are the equity graph slowly increases. Traders make money, give money back, make more money, give some more back, make more money, and give some more back. The key to an equity graph is limiting the losses. Nadex does exactly that -- it limits the losses upfront.

5. Since Nadex offers the capped risk and each option contract has a maximum payout of $100, being undercapitalized is less of an issue. The same $5,000 account in Nadex, with proper money management techniques and sensible trading guidelines, allows for drawdowns. For example, the equity graph below shows hypothetical results after 700 trades, using a $50 maximum loss, a $50 maximum profit, a 52 percent winning percentage rate, and a

$1.80 round trip commission for each trade. The red line shows the drawdown and the blue line shows the profits and losses. The first few trades were rocky and then it evened out. Profits went up and down several times, but steadily the account increased and there was sufficient money in the account to withstand the drawdown of approximately $800.

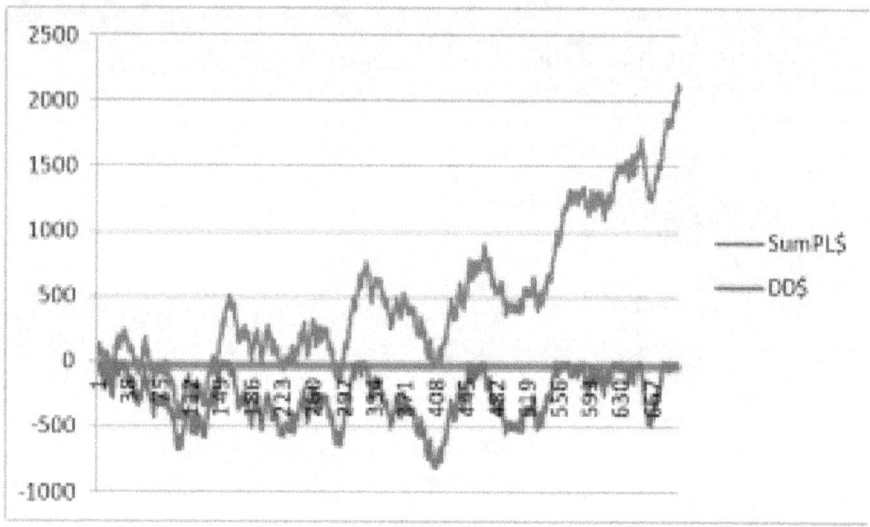

6. Since the trader would not be under-capitalized, his fears would tend to lessen. The trader would be more apt to concentrate on the charts and on the indicators rather than on the DOM (profit/loss window). He would tend to feel more in control of his trade because he cannot be stopped out and the stops cannot be jumped. A loss of $50 is much easier to take than a loss of $300 – both mentally and financially.

7. Sideways markets are not an issue when trading Nadex Binary Options. In fact, markets that are not trending are much easier to trade. For example, the USDJPY market has decreased in volatility substantially in the last few months. On June 4, 2014 (as seen on the chart below), price was at the Average True Range Stop (ATR) with no buying volume (a desirable entry point).

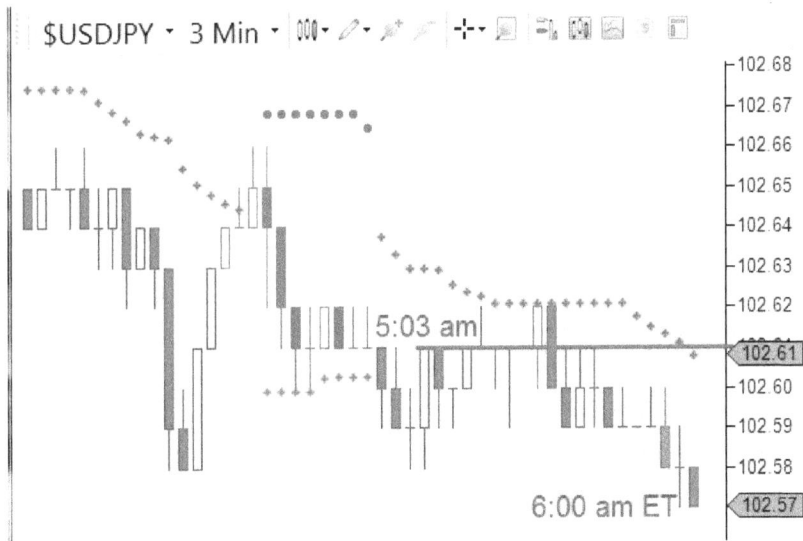

The Nadex Binary Option statement was:

USD/JPY > 102.61 at 6 am ET

Since the trader's bias would be to the downside, he would "sell" the statement (meaning he believed the statement to be false. His risk would be $46 per contract. As you can see from the image below, entering the trade at 5:03 am ET, with an expiration at 6 am ET, price moved down five ticks from the trader's entry point and stayed below 102.61. Within fifty-seven minutes from the time of entry, the trade had a net gain of $92.40 on two contracts after commissions.

Contract			Time Left	Expiry	T...	A...	P...	C...	Profit/Loss
USD/JPY >102.61 (6AM)			2m:27s	04-JUN-14	06/04/14 05:03	54	-2	6.00	$ +96.00

Compare what would have happened if the trader had been trading Futures or Forex contracts.

First, on the spot forex side, the minimum pip spread for the trade would have been at least 1 pip each side or $40 roundtrip (trading two contracts). The margin requirement would have been $2,000. The best-case scenario would be if the trader exited at the low, 102.56 (after the pip spread the trader would have 8 ticks of profit or $80). The worst-case scenario would have been a loss of at least twelve ticks or $120 (pip spread of 1 tick going in and one tick on exit plus a 4 tick stop with two contracts).

On the futures side, the typical margin requirement for the Japanese Yen is $500 per contract ($1,000 for two contracts). A trader would pay $10 minimum round trip for two contracts, and the best-case scenario would be a profit of 8 ticks (4 ticks for each contract) minus commission ($70). The worst-case scenario would be a loss of five ticks per contract plus commission ($110).

Which trade actually gave the trader the highest percentage gain? The highest percentage of gain was with the Nadex Binary Option trade. To enter the option with two contracts was $92 ($46 per option). The profit would be $92.40 after commissions or a net gain of 100.43 percent. On the Spot Forex side, it took $2,000 to make a 4 percent gain. On the futures side, it took $1,000 to make a 7 percent gain.

One could argue that the Nadex Binary Option trade was worse than the futures trade if the Binary Option had lost money. Theoretically it may seem that way. However that would be the maximum loss that the trade could incur. On the futures and Spot Forex side, although you have a stop set, theoretically you can lose more money. For example, if a sudden surge of volatility occurs, price can jump over the stop and keep going thereby exposing the trader to an even higher loss. This does happen. For example, yesterday the G7 meetings were being held in Brussels. Although the meetings were closed to the press, the participants came out of the meeting and made public comments which can cause extreme market volatility. It is for this reason that many traders choose not to trade during the G7 meetings. With Nadex Binary Options, traders can trade during times of market volatility with the confidence that their risk is capped.

Unlike other options, Nadex Binaries are available 24 hours a day, Sunday - Friday, except for 5:00 p.m. – 6:00 p.m. EDT. This means that traders can work their day jobs and still trade during the Asian session (opens at 8:00 p.m. EDT during the summer) or early morning (5:00 a.m. EDT).

In summary, while there are many other advantages, Nadex Binary Options offer traders the ability to trade with smaller accounts, the ability to limit their risk, and the opportunity to avoid the emotional pitfalls that cause many traders to fail. That is why traders love the Nadex Binary Options.

You can learn more about trading the Nadex Binary Options & Spreads in my latest book, A Beginner's Guide: Trading Binaries, and if you are a resident of the USA, Canada, and Mexico, you can open a Nadex account for as little as $100 by visiting http://www.nadex.com

Gail Mercer
www.TradersHelpDesk.com

Chapter 11 - A Basic, Practical and Logical Trade Strategy with Objective Entry, Stop-Loss Placement and Exit Prices By Jaime Johnson

While I can spend your time in this article talking about how a certain indicator works or why bars are better than candlesticks or vice versa, time better spent is getting down to the nitty gritty and showing you a basic trade strategy that you can use right away. While I trade mostly the FOREX markets, this strategy can be used in any market, in any time frame. They are just bars on a chart. While I use bars, candlesticks may also be used. This trade strategy is loosely based on the Elliott Wave Theory, but no wave counts are needed. In my Traders World Presentation, I visually show the following trade strategy as well as discuss current market position of the GBP/USD and the EUR/USD. Here is the basis behind the trade strategy.

1. Trade in the direction of the higher degree time frame oscillator position.

2. Try to get in a trade at or near the end of a correction.

3. Use an oscillator to help to determine the end of the correction.

4. Trade more than one unit.

5. Have a 100% objective entry and stop-loss placement strategy.

In order to get into a position that has potential for some substantial profit, you want to trade in the direction of the higher degree time frame oscillator position. If you enter a trade in a 15 minute chart, the higher degree time frame is the 60 minute time frame. 60M/240M, 240M/Daily, Daily/Weekly, etc. In this example, let's use the 240 minute time frame as the higher degree time frame and the trade entry time frame the 60 minute time frame.

An oscillator is used to determine the momentum direction. Any oscillator may be used, the best ones in my opinion are the Slow Stochastic or the Stochastic RSI. I personally use the DT oscillator which comes with the Dynamic Trader software, it is basically a Stochastic RSI.

Choosing the oscillator setting should be easy and logical. Tweak the oscillator settings so the bearish reversals (when the fast line crosses below the slow line) and bullish reversals (the fast line crosses above the slow line) correlate relatively well with the swing highs and lows of the market. If the past five or so swing highs and lows correlate well with past bearish and bullish reversals of the oscillator, it is a strong possibility the next bearish reversal will correlate with the next swing high and the next bullish reversal will correlate with the next swing low. So if the

240 minute oscillator is oversold or bull, very likely a swing low is at or near completion and the net trend will be sideways to up, so only long positions should be considered in the 60 minute chart. If the 240 minute oscillator is overbought or bear, only short positions may be considered.

In this example, the 240 minute oscillator is bull, only long positions may be considered at this time in the 60 minute chart. Next we are looking for a bearish corrective pattern. Corrections trade against the main trend direction and have an overlapping wave pattern compared to an impulsive or non-overlapping wave pattern. Since only long positions may be considered, we are looking to get in at or near a bearish correction in the 60 minute chart to get into a long trade in the direction of the main bull trend of the higher degree time frame which should resume following the corrective low.

There are few different tools to use to determine when a correction is probably at or near completion. One is using the typical price targets for the end of a correction, the second is using an oscillator in the trade entry time frame. The price targets for a potential corrective low (we are looking to enter a long position) can vary depending on the type of correction unfolding. For this example, we are going to using the general typical price target for a corrective low, the 50% - 61.8% retracement zone of the previous trend range. Choosing the oscillator setting for this time frame is the same procedure as choosing the higher degree time frame oscillator setting. For a potential corrective low, the oscillator very likely will be oversold or bull.

Here is the criteria for the long trade set-up. The 240 minute oscillator must be oversold or bull. In the 60 minute chart we must have a bull trend with impulsive characteristics, followed by a bear corrective pattern. Once the low is in the 50% - 61.8% retracement zone of the bull trend and the 60 minute oscillator is oversold or bull, conditions are in place for a long trade set-up.

Once the criteria for the long trade set-up has been met, there must be an objective place to enter the trade and an objective place for the initial stop-loss. This part must be 100% objective to be able to calculate your risk in a dollar amount in order to calculate your potential maximum loss for the trade and to know how many units you can trade. Unfortunately there is not enough time to get into a detailed money management plan in this article. All I am going to say about this matter is trading is a business and like all successful businesses, money management is a must.

So once the criteria for the long trade set-up is made, a good place to enter the long trade is above the minor swing high prior to the potential corrective low. You can place the stop in one of two places, below the potential corrective low or below the beginning of the bull trend. You probably are saying, "Wait this is not objective, there are two places for my stop." Where you place your stop (below the potential corrective low or below the beginning of the bull trend) will be predetermined in your trade strategy prior to making a trade. If you place your stop below the potential corrective low, the trade will have lower capital exposure. However, it will be a lower probability trade set-up than if you place the stop below the beginning of the bull trend. Placing your stop below the beginning of the bull trend has higher capital exposure, but higher probability. The reason it has higher probability is it gives the trade more room in the event that the corrective low is not yet complete. The only thing that voids a corrective decline to a bull trend is a decline below the beginning of the bull trend.

If a long trade is triggered, a good place to either exit or consider an exit strategy for part of or at least one unit of your long position is at the beginning of the corrective decline. You will secure some profit and you will have at least another long unit in the market for a continued rally. Exit strategies and stop loss adjustment strategies for the remaining part of the long position is subjective and should be dealt with depending on how the market the unfolds.

Are there better corrections to trade than others? The answer is yes, try to trade with the trend. Picking higher degree highs and lows is tricky. If a trend has been bearish for weeks, try to get into bearish positions. However, keep in mind only trade in the direction of higher degree time frame oscillator position. If the weekly trend is bear and you enter trades in the 60M time frame, you can avoid trades when the 240M oscillator is oversold or Bull and only look for short positions when the 240 oscillator is overbought or Bear.

Take a look at Chart 1, the AUD/USD 240 minute chart. The Oct. 3 - Oct. 7 rally has characteristics of a trend followed by a decline off the Oct. 7 high with corrective characteristics. The oscillators are oversold (both lines in the bottom 25% of the oscillator range). Long positions may be considered in the 60 minute chart (Chart 2). A low has been made in the typical price target for a corrective low with the 60 minute oscillators oversold and bull. All criteria have been met for a long trade set-up. There are a couple of places to enter the trade. A rally above the 0.8758 swing high or above the 0.8791 swing high. The latter will have more capital exposure but higher probability. There are a couple of places to place the protective sell-stop, below the last bar at 0.8731 (if a new low is not made) and below the Oct. 3 low at 0.8638. The latter will have more capital exposure but higher probability. The only thing that voids a corrective decline to the Oct. 3-7 rally is a decline below the Oct. 3 low.

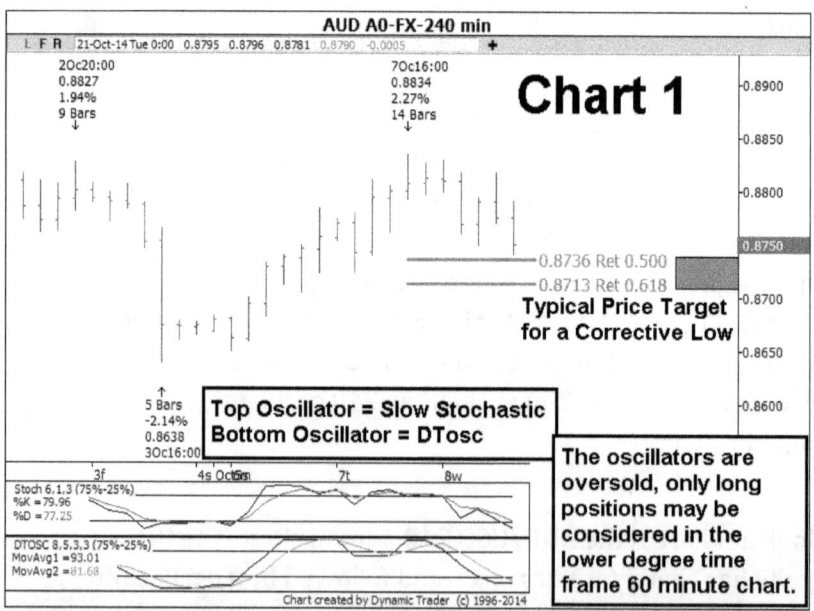

There are many different variations of this strategy such as entering using a trailing one bar high trade strategy or taking profit if the 50% retracement of the corrective decline is reached to secure quicker profit. Which variation you use is not important as long as you stick to the rules of your trade strategy. See my Traders World Online Expo Presentation for further explanation of trading the end of a correction. If you would like to learn more multiple unit and multiple time frame trade entry, exit and stop-loss placement and adjustment strategies as well as a good money management plan, please check out my NoBSFX Workshop at my site. Happy Trading!

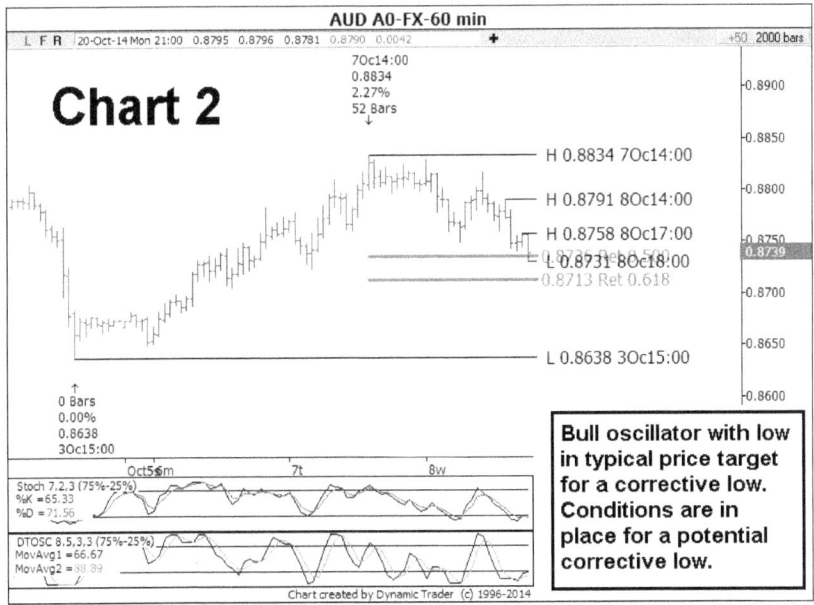

Jaime Johnson
jaime@nobsfxtrading.com
NoBSFX Trading.
www.nobsfx.com

Chapter 12- Multiple Time Frame Trade Strategies by Robert Miner

All trade strategies have the same objective – to identify conditions with a high probability outcome and acceptable capital exposure.

Various approaches to technical analysis are used to identify the conditions with a high probability outcome. Objective trade strategies and position size are used to determine the acceptable capital exposure.

In the past 30 years, I've developed the Dynamic Trading approach described in my book High Probability Trading Strategies to identify trade setups. I've developed a synergistic approach to multiple time frame price, pattern, time and momentum strategies that identify high probability outcome trade setups.

In this article, you will see a recent example of this approach and how it is applicable to any market and any time frame for short term to position trades.

Multiple Time Frame (MTF) analysis looks at a higher and lower time frame to identify when both time frames are in the same position which gives the trader a huge advantage from traders who only consider one time frame of chart. By using at least two time frames, this approach usually identifies trade setups with minimal capital exposure.

Chart #1: S&P Oct. 2014: Dual-Time-Frame Momentum Bear Reversal

In this first example, we will consider the weekly and daily data of the S&P. The MTF momentum setup for a bear trend is when the weekly momentum is Bear and the daily momentum makes a BearRev (Bear Reversal) above the DTosc (Dynamic Trader Oscillator) mid-line. At this dual-time-frame momentum setup, the daily momentum becomes Bear when the higher time frame weekly momentum is Bear which is a high probability setup for an immediate continuation of the higher time frame weekly Bear trend.

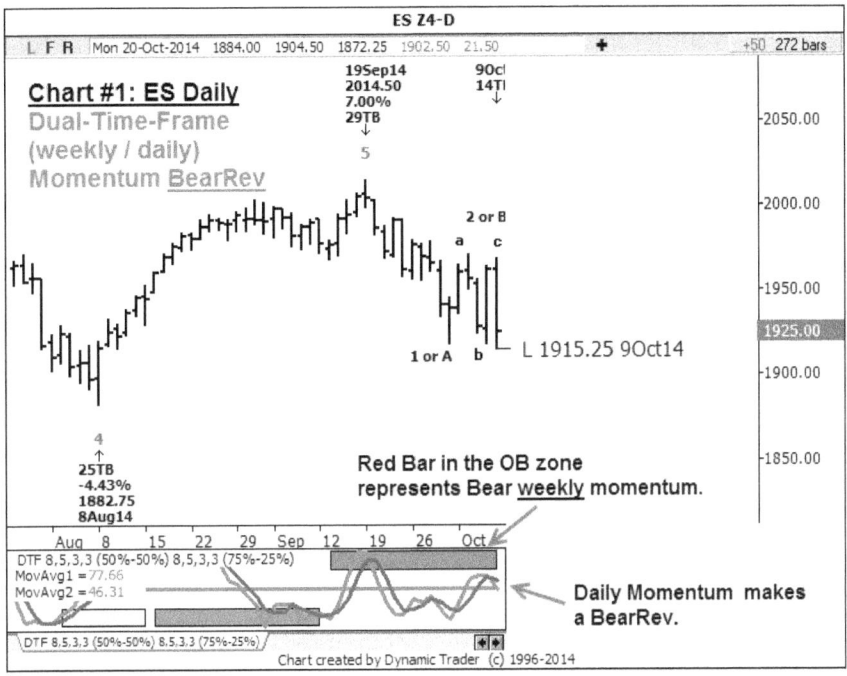

On Oct. 9, the last bar on the ES daily chart, the weekly momentum was Bear as represented by the red bar in the OB zone of the indicator window and the daily momentum made a BearRev. This is a Dual-Time-Frame Momentum Reversal setup for a continuation of the Bear trend. The odds are high that the ES had completed an ABC correction and will immediately continue the Bear trend for at least several days.

Chart #2: Dual-Time-Frame Momentum Extreme OS (Over Sold)

Four days later, the ES had declined over 100 points to reach the price target zone for a reversal. More importantly, when the price zone was reached on Oct. 15, the weekly momentum was now OS (over sold) and the daily momentum was extreme OS warning at least a daily if not weekly low was near. This setup alerts the trader who is short to trail stops very close to the market and prepare for a long trade.

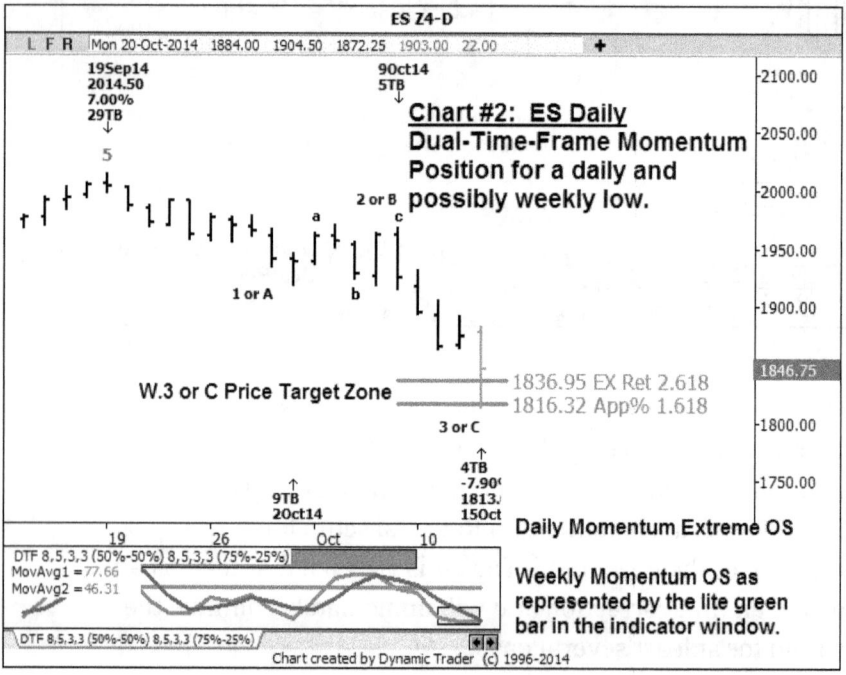

Traders can either wait for a daily momentum BullRev (Bull Reversal) when the two higher time frames of momentum are OS or go to smaller time frame data for the momentum BullRev for a triple time frame momentum reversal setup to exit short positions and enter long positions. The next chart shows the 60m Dual-Time-Frame Momentum Reversal setup at Multiple-Time-Frame Price Support to exit a short trade and enter a long trade with minimal capital exposure.

Chart #3: Dual-Look back Momentum Bull Reversal Trade Setup

As of the end of the day of Oct. 15, the ES was in a Dual-Time-Frame weekly/daily OS momentum position to complete a daily and possibly weekly low. Instead of waiting until the end of the following day, Thursday, Oct. 16 for a daily momentum BullRev to complete the trade setup, go to a lower time frame ID (IntraDay) setup for a trade setup with minimum capital exposure.

A 60m Dual-Look back Momentum Reversal setup with price at ST EOW (End Of Wave) price target zone which overlapped the higher time frame price support is a Triple-Time-Frame setup (weekly/daily/60m) for a long trade.

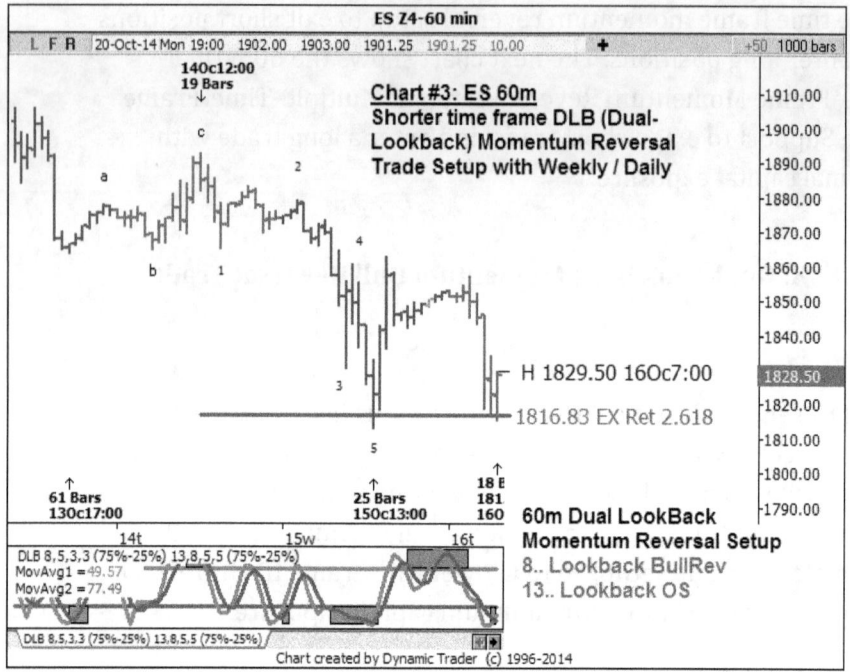

A Dual-Look Back (DLB) Momentum Reversal is when the shorter look back momentum oscillator makes a BullRev while the longer look back momentum is OS. This is very similar to a Dual-Time-Frame Momentum Reversal Setup but uses two look back periods instead of two distinct time periods. A Dual-Look back Momentum Reversal during a Dual-Time-Frame Momentum extreme is a setup that can't be ignored and usually results in a trade setup with very little capital exposure.

The entry and initial protective sell-stop are completely objective. Once the DLB momentum reversal is made, enter on a buy stop one tick above the price bar made at the DLB setup with a stop no further then the immediate swing low prior to the setup.

Chart #4: ES Daily

As of the day this article is written (Oct. 20), the ES is up over 80 points since the Multiple-Time-Frame momentum and price setup for an ES long trade on Oct. 16. The daily momentum is not yet OB so the assumption is the advance is not complete and has further to go.

Every MTF and DLB setup is not going to result in an immediate and major trend. In some cases, the entry will never be hit if the prior trend continues without making the anticipated reversal. In other cases, the entry will be elected with no follow through and the trade will be stopped out. The significant advantage of MTF setups is the initial capital exposure is usually very low if the trade does not work out. The other advantage is you are entering following a lower time frame reversal for a higher time frame trend which usually has significantly greater profit potential than the initial capital exposure. In the case of this setup and entry, you are trading for a daily trend which usually lasts 3-5 days on a 60m setup with very little initial capital exposure relative to the daily trend objectives.

Make Multiple-Time-Frame Trade Strategies The Basis of Your Trading Plan

This is not just a well chosen, after the fact example. This exact setup was described in our DT Reports as it was made.

In the DT Futures and DT Stock/ETF Reports we focus on identifying Multiple-Time-Frame and Dual-Look back setups for the major financial markets and stock sectors and component stocks for short term to position trades.

In the Traders World recorded webinar that accompanies this book, we illustrate many other examples of a wide variety of markets to teach you more about this unique approach to technical analysis and trade strategies.

After 30 years of trading and teaching traders, I have refined this approach to identify high probability trade setups for any market and any time frame.

Robert Miner is the author of High Probability Trading Strategies and the Dynamic Trader Software and Trading Course and publishes the DT Futures and DT Stock/ETF Reports. For more information, go to www.DynamicTraders.com.

Robert Miner
bob@dynamictraders.com

Dynamic Traders Group, Inc.
www.DynamicTraders.com

Chapter 13- Should I Trade Today? By Adrienne Toghraie

If you honestly answered this question every day and traded only on your peak performance days, your annual gross income would exceed anything you have ever produced. This is assuming, of course, that you have and are following a good trading plan. The chances are that most of you do not want to ask this question because you will trade regardless of the answer. The objective is to minimize your risk and maximize your potential for taking successful action. The way to accomplish this is to follow your trading system faithfully, which should require that you trade only when you are in a peak state of physical and emotional readiness.

Self-Deception

Neil lies to himself about his ability to trade on the days that he should be doing something else. The resulting trading sessions usually incur losses that require significant time for him to recover lost trading momentum. What Neil wants to know is why he persists in trading when he should know better. Since Neil is not the only trader who trades in self-deception, it is important to understand why this happens and what a trader can do to prevent it.

Bad Trading Days

Let's face it, we all have good days and bad days. But, traders are not like stage actors who have to perform despite wracking fevers, sprained ankles, and broken hearts. While an actor's career depends upon his showing up and giving his best performance for a paying audience every day. A trader simply cannot rely on memory and rehearsal to make it through days when he feels bad because the play of the market is never the same from moment to moment. In an instant of miscalculation, emotional weakness, or lack of focus, a trader can suffer a crippling loss with long-term consequences. These lapses are most likely to occur, not when you are at the top of your form, but when you are off your feed.

At the very least, there will be days when you simply did not get enough sleep, missed taking your allergy medicine, or are coming down with a cold. While these conditions are physical and moderate, they have a definite and measurable effect on your ability to think and take action: your brain is not as quick, your perceptions are dulled, your reaction-time is longer and your decisions are not first-rate.

While they are not actually sick or in pain, there are also a fair number of traders who are never at their physical peak. These traders are the ones who hit the bars after work, abuse drugs, eat unhealthy diets, and either over-exercise or are permanently adhered to the sofa cushions. Banking on their youth and strong constitutions, they may not have really bad days, but they will not trade to their full potential even if they are showing good performance.

If moderate physical changes can have a significant impact on your trading edge, imagine the profound impact of severe physical challenges! I have worked with traders who are trying to make major trading decisions on days when they are suffering from migraine headaches, severe back pain, unrelenting arthritic pain, injury or post-operative recuperation. A handful of traders can actually use their pain to enhance their focus and can trade better as a result. These traders are the exception. For most of us mortals, severe pain and discomfort drain off energy, focus, and commitment to our self-disciplines. It gets harder and harder to follow your system when you are trying to survive physically.

When Everything Goes Wrong

Not all bad trading days result from physical consequences. Emotional and personal factors can also be the cause of potentially disastrous trading days. Traders facing a personal crisis such as a divorce, a death in the family, or the loss of a close friend should not be trading. Over the past several years, I have repeatedly cautioned traders who were going through a personal crisis to stop trading. Marital conflict is one of the most common causes for bad trading days. A trader who has just decided to leave his wife and family or is in the middle of a stressful divorce is often looking at months of bad trading days. It is difficult to convince such a trader that he can afford to stop trading. Unfortunately, his trading often becomes very costly during this time.

When Everything Goes Right

On the other hand, a reason for not trading can be the day after a major win in the markets when a trader can be too emotionally over-charged with ego and greed to make good decisions. When everything goes right and everything seems wonderful and happy, a trader can experience a tremendous drain on his focus and attention. The reasons could be when a new baby is on the way, a family reunion is being planned, a wedding is in the works, when you are blissfully in love or lust, or when you are building a new house.

Filtering Reality

What makes a day unfit for trading is when a trader's emotional or physical condition filters out the information normally received in making good trading decisions. The result is that trading rules are not followed. Once normal perceptions are altered, reactions, regardless of how good or bad they are, will not match normal, good decisions.

How to Decide

So, you are convinced that it is a good idea to ask yourself each day whether you should go to bat today or sit on the sidelines and wait out the game. But, how do you make the decision? Based on what criteria? Below is a list of questions that could be helpful in making the decision. Each day is different so that one question might be relevant today, but not tomorrow.

Jim, one of my clients, copied this list, changed some questions to make them more relevant to his own life, added some questions, and pasted it on his bathroom mirror. Each morning before he finished shaving, he reviewed the list. To his surprise, Jim found that he could not get through the list without disqualifying himself at least one day a week. When he gave himself permission to not trade when he was off his form, he found that he had more energy, enthusiasm, and focus when he returned to trading. As a result, his drawdowns were lessened and he was able to pick better trades to enter and ride to their end-game.

Here is the list that I have developed. If a question strikes you as not useful to your situation, simply eliminate it and add your own. At the very least, find one or two that work for you and make them a part of your daily routine.

On a scale of one to ten, with one being the most awful and ten being the most energetic and healthy, how do I feel today:

a. Physically?

b. Mentally?

c. Emotionally?

(Anything lower than a 6 cannot be described as a peak performance day.)

Is there something on my mind that has me concerned, distressed, upset, angry, panicked or feeling very guilty, so that I can't seem to stop thinking about it?

Did I just have a major win in the market? One that has me over the top? (If yes, read your business plan and tighten up on your risk if you have a rollercoaster issue of losing after major wins.)

Did I just have a major loss in the market? One that has major implications for me? (If yes, ask yourself, did I follow my rules? If yes, pat yourself on the back. If not, ask yourself what lesson have I learned? Then pat yourself on the back for deciding to not make that mistake again.)

Did I just win in the markets by <u>not</u> following my rules? If so, realize that you are either going to have to change your rules, or accept the fact that it was a mistake and not to repeat that behavior again.

Did a major event happen in my life recently, either positively or negatively? (If so, notice how that event has affected your energy and emotions. Pull back from the day's trading if your behavior is different from what it normally is.)

Have I been experiencing a series of losses in the market? (If yes, take time for a periodic review of your business plan and make sure you are aware of any changes in the market. Adjust your plan to accommodate any changes.)

Did I break my good routines yesterday? This can include failing to take care of yourself such as your exercise routine, your eating disciplines, overdoing alcohol, not sleeping, etc. (Consider anything above a four as a day to stay on the bench.)

Could I concentrate on a game of chess (use your favorite game of strategy and concentration) right now in order to beat an opponent as good as I am at my very best? (If not, you're not good enough to compete with the big boys in the market today.)

Did I wake up feeling that I needed four more hours of sleep? (If your morning routine includes a good breakfast protein dish, exercise, and meditation, you can leave the house feeling fully energized. This is not an issue, but you need to question whether you can willingly risk the family money if you leave the house exhausted.)

It is 11:00 in the morning or 2:00 in the afternoon. Would you give anything to close your eyes for a while? (If so, you should not be trading.)

During the trading day, if anything happens that would bring you to the negative part of any of the above situations, you might have to quit at that point in the trading day and not wait until the next day.

No Shame in Not Trading

So, you see the kind of questions that you should be asking yourself: what is your mental and physical preparation for the day? Once you review this list, you might find yourself saying, "Okay, maybe I'm not at my best today, but so what? I trade when I'm feeling bad and I usually manage to get through the day without a catastrophe. If I waited to trade when I felt wonderful, I'd never trade. This is a lot of hooey." If you find yourself responding this way, you will have a lot of company. I have seen countless traders who are convinced that they can trade regardless of how they feel. But, I wish you could see them after they decide that they are going to sideline themselves on those low-energy days. Once a trader takes control of his trading on this new level, he finds that he trades better than ever before. It is only after trying this strategy that traders are able to honestly look at their performance and see the strain on their trading from the long-term habit of trading when unfit. If you force yourself through the first rough day, are you doing any better the second day?

There is no shame in not trading when you should not be trading. This concept is one that you should cozy up to if your goal is to reach the next level of trading mastery and success. And by the way, those traders who have the discipline to take themselves out of the game when they are not up to par have fewer days they have to do so because they figure out ways to prevent occurrences

Getting in Shape to Trade

The best way to insure that you can answer the question of whether or not you should trade today is to be disciplined. The routines of self-discipline that address your physical and emotional well-being are your best defense against bad trading days. They are also the means to insure that you follow your trading disciplines, as well. If you find yourself answering the checklist in the negative column, chances are good that you have been breaking your disciplines. Your disciplines may not be able to protect you from some of the major shocks in life such as divorce or death of someone close to you, but they can give you the strength to weather these shocks and return to your trading sooner.

Conclusion

Because successful, long-term trading requires you to be at your peak each day that you trade, there will be many days when you should not be trading. Unlike many professions in which you can coast through your bad days, a bad day in trading can mean the end of a career at worst and unexpected losses at best. Simply by asking yourself honestly each day whether or not you should be trading and keeping yourself out of the game if your answer is "No" can vastly improve your trading results.

Adrienne Toghraie, Trader's Success Coach
Adrienne@TradingOnTarget.com
TradingOnTarget.com
TradingOnTarget.com

Chapter 14- Degrees of the Market by Sean McKissen

How can trading be so hard when the market can only go up or down? On the surface it would seem that anyone would have a 50/50 chance of success at any given time by going long or short. The reality is the success rate is much lower than 50%, but why?

I have been trading for 20 years and the answer to the above question did not come easily. Like you I used to think MACD and fast momentum indicators were my answer, but in reality all they did was cause me mass confusion. The five minute indicators would tell me price was going higher but then it would reverse back down and the market would have a huge sell-off. It didn't make sense to me why the five minute indicators were right some of the time but wrong most of the time.

After watching the charts for many years I saw that there are different degrees on one time frame and there are different degrees using multiple time frames. Multiple time frame degrees are an easier concept to learn because it makes sense that the five minute timeframe is trading inside the sixty minute timeframe because the five minute is a smaller time frame.

The confusion most people have is the different degrees of the market on just one time frame. To learn this you have to be very specific with your thought process.

Below is a good starting point for your core thinking of how waves and patterns are built in the markets.

1. Multiple bars equal one wave

2. Multiple minor waves equal a major wave

3. Multiple waves equal one pattern

Inside of one wave there will be multiple smaller waves (minor wave) to the one bigger wave. Seeing this will give you a good example of how two degrees are happening at one time. An easy visual is the chart below. You will see the price pulls down into the major buy box and then the wave goes up. Inside of the one wave up (noted by the blue line) there were smaller degrees of up and down waves noted buy the price rotating the green line. This is a good example of three degrees on one chart all at the same time.

Major (Blue box)

Medium (Blue line)

Minor (Green line) What is the value of knowing this?

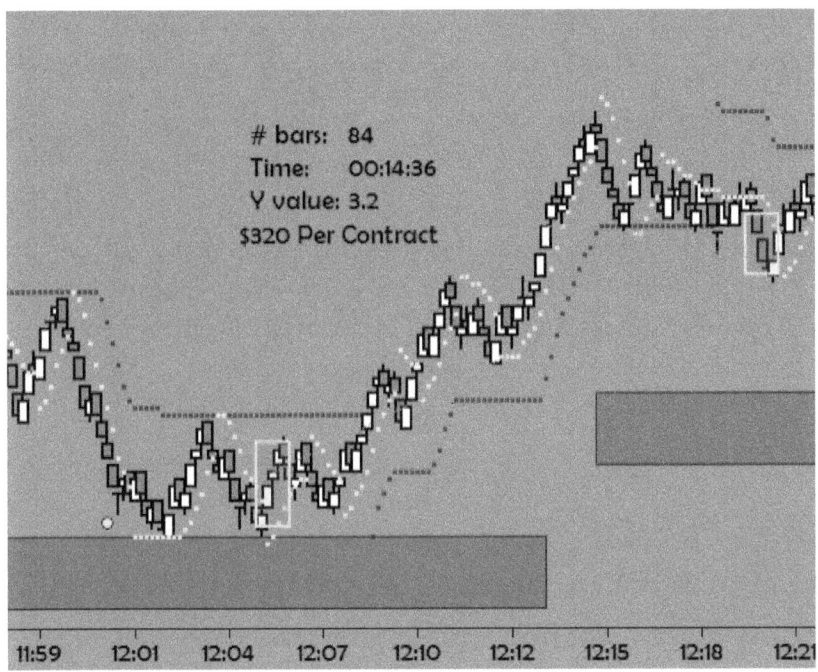

The goal in trading is to have the smallest stops with the biggest profit opportunity.

It is easy to make this part of your trading plan but how are you achieving this? The rules to achieve this have to be absolute based off repeatable structure, not part of your gut feeling.

The only way to have small stops with big rewards is to be specific with how you label the charts and know what degree you are trading and why. If you enter a trade with a major stop but only a minor profit target your risk to reward will always be off. Doing this you will add pressure on yourself to have to be right on 90% of your trades which is very hard to do. Even if you are right on 90% do you hold the profitable trades long enough to make it worth the risk?

We want to avoid the pressure and frustration of the market and stick to absolute rules based on degrees and waves that duplicate. Once we have the confidence in our entry and how we manage the risk, we can then go to the next step which is learning the direction of the market, where you want to enter and when you want to enter.

No matter if you are a swing trader, day trader or scalper. It does not matter the time frame or the symbol the natural wave structure of the markets move in minor and major degrees.

In our opinion no lagging indicator will ever tell you the structure or degree of the markets which are the two most important aspects of trading.

If you want to learn more and see how we trade live join us in our live room 100% for free.

To learn more go to www.360wallst.com and join our free email list and you will get all the invites to the live room and advanced wave structure training for free!

Sean Mckissen
mckissen333@yahoo.com
360Wallst
http://www.360wallst.com/

Chapter 15- Trading Stocks Using Market Profile and Auction Market Principles by Tom Alexander

Why do stocks, and stock indices, go up and down? Is it based on a perception of value? Is it momentum? Let's address each potential reason in more depth.

If stocks move up or down based on the perception of value, then how is value being measure? Is there a universal standard among stock market analysts regarding a true and standard definition of value? I think we can agree there is certainly not a single definition of value among analysts and institutional types. As the saying goes, this is what makes a market; one analyst thinks a stock is "undervalued" and a different analyst thinks a stock is "overvalued". Both analysts can likely make a well researched and reasoned outline *using the same financial metrics* to make their opposing opinions about whether or not a stock should be moving higher or lower. How helpful to the trader can that possibly be? How reliable can that method of analysis possibly be?

How about momentum? We hear all the time that a stock is going up only because, well, it's going up. These are derisive comments almost always attributable to the financial value analyst who was on the other side of the trade/analysis. Someone is finding value in the stock or they would not be buying it, even if that value IS just because it is going up.

What if there was a way to come up with an objective, universal of VALUE? Wouldn't that make trading and analysis much easier? Well, there is. Auction Market Principles describe how and why stocks (and all other assets that trade in an auction environment) do what they do. Auction Market Principles are based on logical concepts of market movement:

The Purpose of a Market is to Facilitate Trade

The sole purpose of an auction market is to give buyers and sellers the opportunity to do business. This is affected through a transparent process of price discovery. Trade is most efficiently facilitated when there is a general agreement on VALUE between the buyer and seller – a range is established with relatively little activity at the upper and lower extremes of the range and most of the activity at the mode of the range. It is the mode of the range that offers the fairest price to both the buyer and seller.

All Stocks Follow a Predictable Pattern of Development

Trade facilitation creates a consistent development process all stocks follow. Step 1: The stock trends Step 2: A range is established and stocks stay in stay in that range as long as the perception of VALUE remains unchanged. Step 3: The perception of VALUE changes and the stock begins to trend, with either the buyers or sellers clearly in control.

Below is a chart of Facebook. FB stayed in a range from June 2012 until July 2013. This was "Balance" in which there was a general consensus of VALUE. In July of 2013 FB began trending higher.

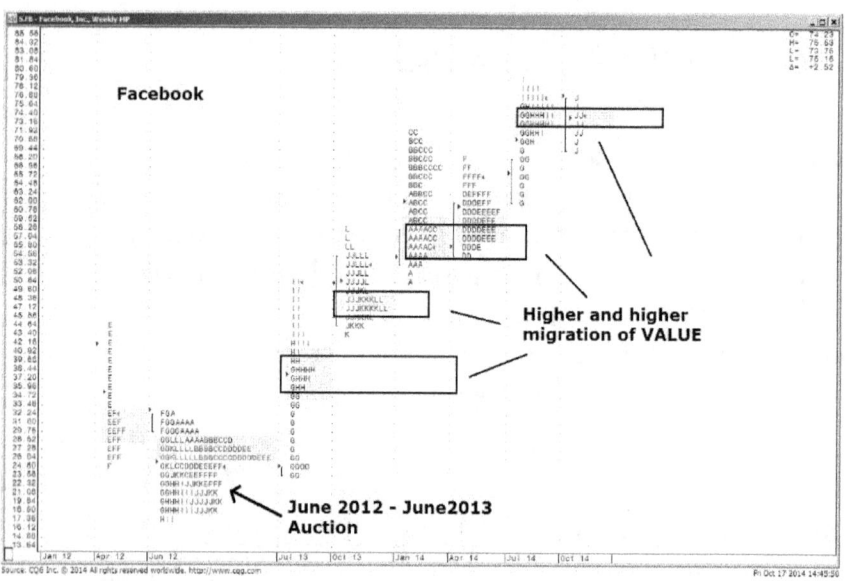

VALUE is Determined Solely by the Market Participants

In Auction Market Analysis, VALUE has a single, objective definition: VALUE is whatever the general consensus between the buyers and sellers suggest it should be based entirely on their actions. The more trade activity and time spent in a given range the more the market is finding VALUE in that range of prices.

There is no debate of what VALUE should be such as you find with other forms of analysis, whether fundamental or technical. It is what the market says it is. It is by far the most objective and consistent way of determining VALUE.

In the chart below of AT&T is is clear the market has found the most VALUE from about 34.50 to 36.00. That area is the "High Volume Node" where the greatest amount of trade activity has occurred over the past two and one half years.

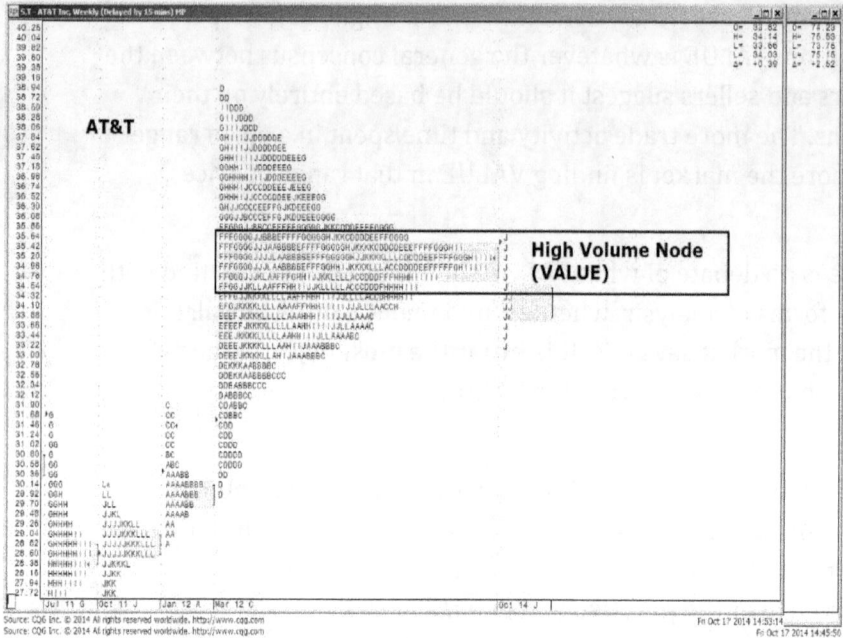

The benefit of being able to determine what VALUE is (and is not) can lead to the development of any number of trade plans that have a positive expectancy. These concepts can be helpful:

Price is Regressive from the Extremes of an Established Range

This is true as long as the perception of VALUE in a given range has not changed. Trades can be taken near the upper and lower extreme of the range offering a relatively large potential reward to the amount of risk that has to be assumed to take the trade.

All Balance Eventually Breaks into Imbalance

A stock will stay in a range until there is a perception on the part of either the buyers or sellers that the present consensus of VALUE is changing. At that point either the buyers or sellers will take control of the stock and it will trend. That starts over again the three step process described above. Being alert for this break can offer the ideal trade and help the trader get on board a stock when it is just begging a substantial move.

The Auction Market Three Step Process Applies to All Degrees of Time

This fact is one of the primary reasons this is such an extraordinarily robust approach to analysis and trading. The exact same process of development occurs on the intraday charts as on daily and weekly charts. This often produces the opportunity to have the risk on an intraday structure but the potential reward of a much larger degree time frame.

In the charts of Alibaba below several of the above concepts are displayed. In the first chart we can see BABA traded in a range from 10/3 to 10/9. Each day ultimately combined to form one auction, or Balance Area that encompassed a price range of 87.00 - 90.30.

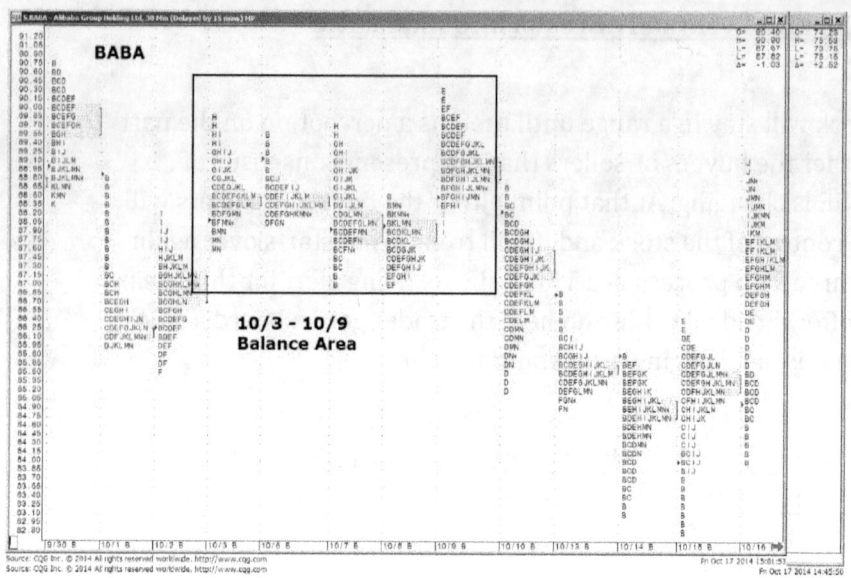

In the second chart of BABA we have combined the 10/3 – 10/9 range into one auction. On 10/10 the Balance Area broke and a trend down began.

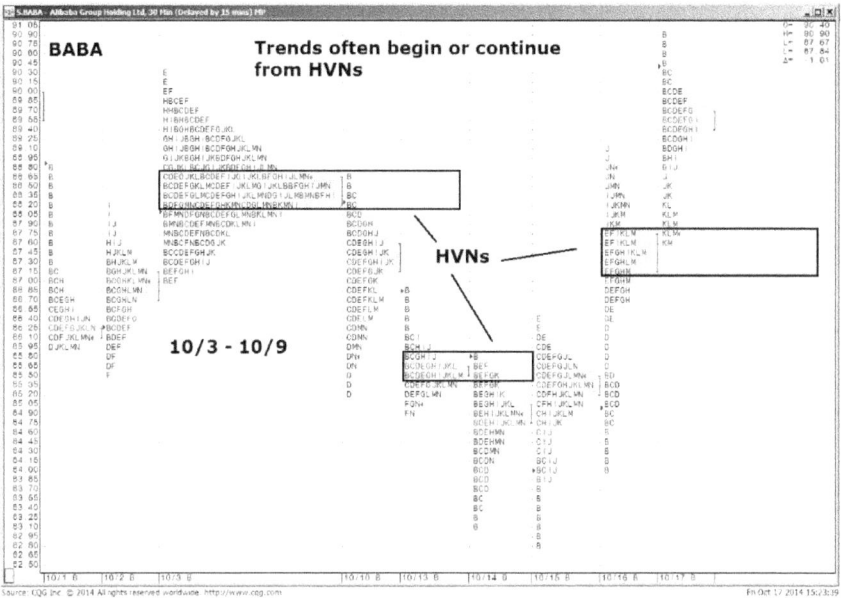

These charts illustrate the fractal nature of the Auction process. If you look closely you can see the same basic shapes of each day that then combine to form the larger degree Balance Area of 10/3 – 10/9. We can go even further down in time frame to a 5-minute intraday chart and see the same shapes as the larger degree auction. What this is displaying is the Auction Process of development that is occurring in all degrees of time, all the time!

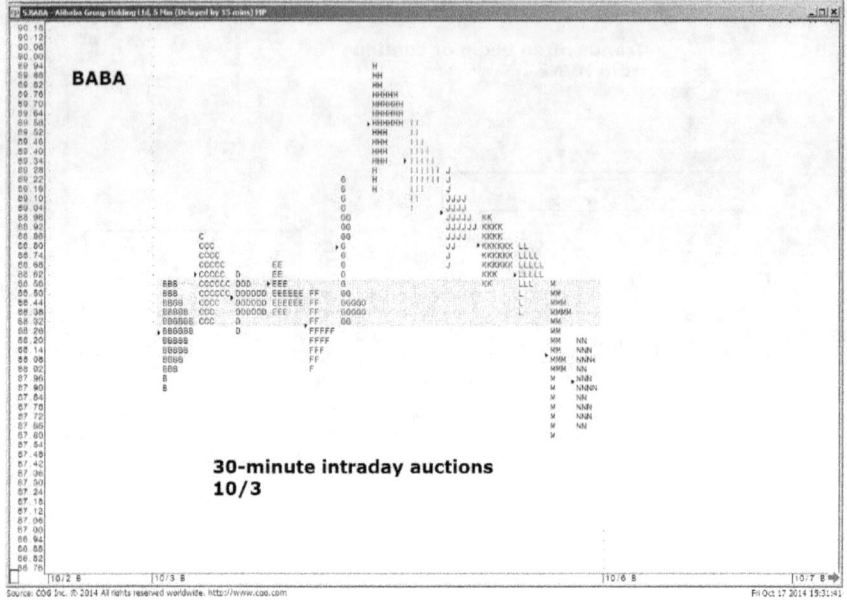

30-minute intraday auctions
10/3

The Signal of a Change in Trend is Objectively Determined by the Migration of VALUE

The path of least resistance and the side of the market one should be favoring is in the direction of the larger degree migration of Value. It is both unnecessary and unwise to play pick the top/bottom in markets. This methodology provides a consistent way of determining the larger degree trend and when they trend is probably reversing.

In the chart of Apple below we see the clear migration of VALUE upward through the September auction. The High Volume Node for October is forming below the HVN of September and therefore is an initial signal of a trend change.

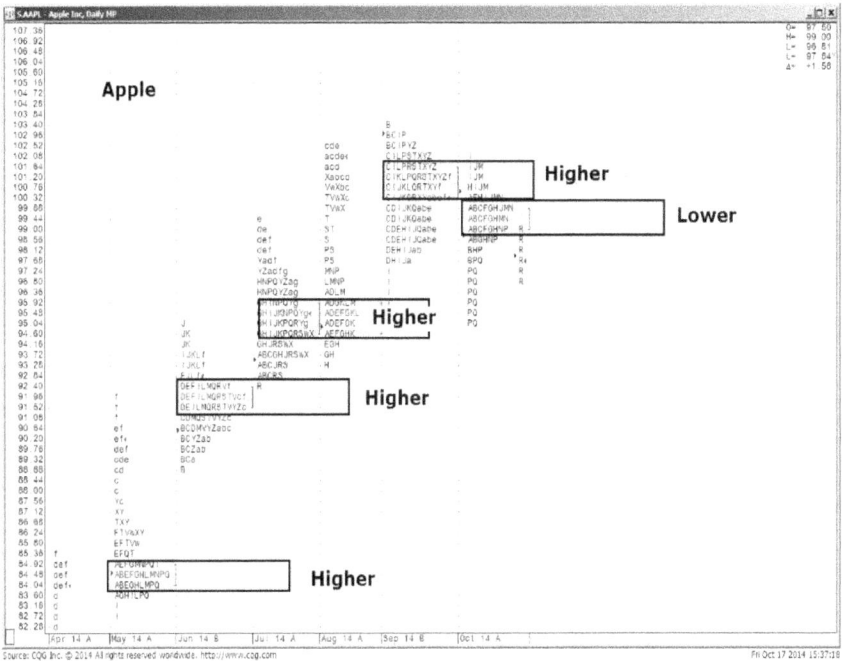

Hopefully you can see the potential for using this methodology in your trading. Obviously, there is much more to this methodology than can be presented in a brief article and video presentation. If you would like a free course in using these concepts please visit our website at www.AlexanderTrading.com.

Tom Alexander
tom@alexandertrading.com

Alexander Trading
www.alexandertrading.com

Chapter 16- Great Tips on Buying the Right Trading Computer by Larry Jacobs

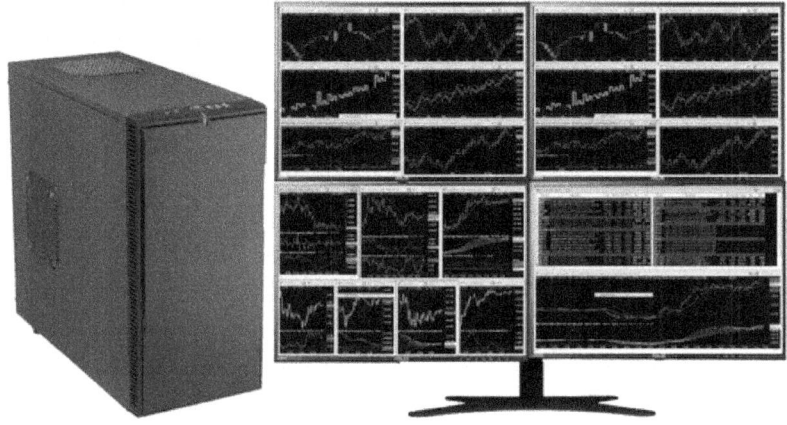

1) A trader is unlike an investor because he buys and sells in the market frequently to capture gains from the swings. He generally does it by using minute, hourly, daily, weekly and monthly charts. The successful traders first tests their systems on historical data before they trade. Then when the system is confirmed that it is successful they start trading it slowly and then will tweak it until it is even much better.

2) The successful trader uses top of the line trading software. There are many out there. For example, TradeStation,

NinjaTrader, MetaStock are some of the favorites to mention a few.

3) The successful trader uses a fast, reliable, and quiet trading computer so he can make quick and profitable decisions. All three of these are necessary for success. None is more important than the computer. Most traders don't understand the difference between trading computers. The successful traders do understand the importance of a quality trading computer.

This section of the book will give you the knowledge to get the right customized computer that will fit you and give you many years of a reliable service. This is from my personal view as I am best qualified to explain this. I have been in business since 1986 selling trading computers and I have watched the trends and the evolution of the computer. I have studied the various trading computer sites. I have questioned our Traders World subscribers that have purchased trading computers and I understand what they need. See the Sonata Trading Computer here. How Many Monitors to Use Most traders start out with generally two monitors because they have a beginning approach to trading and they don't know what to do with more monitors. Experienced successful traders will generally have 4 to 8 monitors. If you are a beginning trader you should purchase a computer that might support two or three monitors expandable to up to 8 monitors later on. Our computer out of the box supports three trading monitors even without a video card. The motherboard we use can support 3 monitors using an internal Intel Graphics processor. So if you just want 2-3 monitors just stay with the onboard graphics.

Later on if you want more than 3 monitors you can order 1 or 2 video cards which support 4 monitors each or a total of 8.CPUs

The CPU is perhaps the most important part of the computer. It gives the computer its maximum potential. It works with the motherboard chipset to give you ultimate power you need to trade with. Generally there are two versions of a CPU. One is the low end with a set maximum speed and the other one is the high end usually noted with a K after the number. The higher end model is capable with the right motherboard to overclock to higher speeds.

Most mass produced computers always have the low end CPUs in them and they never have a motherboard capable of overclocking. There are three important aspects to consider selecting a CPU.

The Family of the Processor

The current Intel family is the Haswell and the prior was the Ivy Bridge. The Haswell runs 10% faster and runs cooler than the previous family, the Ivy Bridge. If a CPU runs too hot it will many times force the CPU to what is called thermal throttling. What that means is the computer slows down to lower the temperature to protect itself from burning up. You don't want your CPU to slow down when you need the extra speed for example when the market takes off and puts stress on your computer. The only way to overcome that problem is to put a better cooler on the CPU. We use two types of CPU coolers, the air type and the liquid type.

of Threads

The number of threads is important. CPUs are different in the number for cores it uses. Each core of a CPU can process an instruction. So the more cores it has the faster it can do calculations if the software supports it. If a program is written with multiple threads then each thread can use a different core to do the job. So if you use a CPU that will handle more threads and the program is written for the more threads then it will get the job done faster. You need to know about the program details to see if having more cores will give you more speed.

What is different between the i5 and the i7 CPU?

The difference is that the i7 has what is called hyper threading and that allows calculations to be done separately from others therefore increasing the number of threads. That means that an i7 has eight threads (4 for math and 4 for non-math calculations)

Processor Speed

Speed is the final thing to consider in selecting the CPU. If the program you are using is non-threaded then you would want the fastest CPU speed possible. If you have more speed it will help to eliminate lockups when the market takes off and makes a big move. Intel just released a new CPU, the i7-4790K Quad Core which runs at a minimum of 4.0GHz and can be overclocked to 4.6GHz and runs cooler on top of that.

Overclocking

Overclocking can be used to increase the speed of a CPU if you have a high quality motherboard. If done incorrectly you can decrease the life of the CPU. Many of the trading computer manufactures advertise that their computers are overclocked and run much faster. To get many motherboards to overclock a CPU you have to be a trained CPU tech. So if you get one of these computers that are overclocked, it is all setup by the manufacture in the BIOS by a technician. If you for some reason lose the BIOS setting, you are out of luck. The speed goes back to the base speed of the CPU. By the way you can easily lose your BIOS setting just be having your computer lock up and when you reboot it the old BIOS is gone.

You can optimize your computer by yourself; you no longer need a technician. The Sonata Trading Computer uses an Asus high end motherboard that with the push of one button you get 5-way optimization by dual processors. With this you get performance, efficiency, stable digital power, unbeatable fan control and even networking and audio tuning optimized for you. With this technology trading programs run smoothly with high performance, prioritized bandwidth and vivid sound. Fans stay whisper-quiet for daily trading and extreme cool when the markets speed up. Energy waste is reduced so you'll save money. This one button optimizer uses the most intuitive UEFI Bios. The mouse – controlled graphical BIOS is made for both the PC novice and the seasoned over clocker. The EZ and the Advanced Modes help you find you way quickly and easily. You don't have to be a computer technician to figure it out. Just push one button!

There are two types of CPU coolers:

The Air Type

The air type cools the CPU by blowing air through the cooling fins of the unit. The above unit is the best-selling and the popular unit out there. We recommend this as a minimum on your computer. Trading computers run much faster than normal computers and usually need a better cooling system than the stock Intel CPU. Both the enhanced large air and liquid coolers do a much better job. Which is better, the liquid is the best and little more expensive, but both do the job.

The Liquid Type

The liquid type blows are through a radiator and the cool liquid flows around the CPU heat sink. This is a 2nd option and is better than the air-type above. The Stock Intel CPU Cooler The Intel CPU is just the bare minimum. Power Supplies The power supplies in many stock computers are generally around 250 watts and are not capable of supporting multiple monitors. A trading computer needs a minimum of 500 watts and up to 750 watts is even better. A bigger power supply will not be stressed and will last much longer. Power supplies use capacitors. The quality of the capacitors is extremely important. The cheap power supplies use liquid capacitors which dry out and eventually fail.

It is also important that the power supply is certified Active PFC compatible. All of ours are Active PFC compatible. That means it won't run at full power all the time and waste electricity, but will only use the power required. Also it is important that it be nearly silent. You as a trader need your full concentration to be successful trading the markets. The higher quality power supplies also have more amps which is needed for more powerful motherboards and video cards that our Sonata Trading Computer have. The cheaper ones don't have that amp power and are constantly stressed and that is why they fail so much. Computer Memory When the first computers came out They only used 1 GB of memory. Half of it was used for the operating system and the rest for software. Now you need at least a minimum of 8GB of memory and it is recommended to go to either 16 or 32GB.

Memory usage works better if you shut the computer down nightly. If you don't shut it down every night then you might go to 32GB in your machine. You will also need Windows 7 Pro to run 32GB.

The best memory we have found is the Corsair Vengence. The current specifications on the memory we use right now is 1866MHz 9-10-9-27 1.5V for Intel Dual Channel Processor platforms. There generally 4 slots on motherboards, so you can use 2 – 4GB modules, 2 – 8GB modules or 4 – 8GB modules. The Corsair Vengence memory works nicely on the Intel platforms with outstanding performance and stability. Each module is built carefully with selected DRAM to allow for excellent overclocking performance. They have a limited lifetime warranty. We use it in all of our trading computers.

Video Cards

Concerning video cards you want a card that is reliable and powerful yet silent. Most video cards fitting this category are few and far between. There are basically two main video card makers: ATI and Nvidia. Both are good. The cards of today have different types of outputs: DVI, Display Port, Mini-Display Port, HDMI, mini HDMI and the VGA. To work all of these must connect to the monitor types of connections: VGA, DVI, Display Port and HDMI. Sometimes it is necessary to using adapters to make this transition. This is a HDMI to DVI adapter.

The video card that we use in the Sonata Trading Computer is the Asus GT640 Silent. That means there are no noisy fans. Fans also wear out and then the card burns up. Because this card does not have a fan and uses Direct CU cooling, it will last much longer than a regular video card with fans. It will also power four monitors. We can put two of these video cards in the Sonata and it will support eight monitors. The high end Asus motherboard we use has the ability to support three monitors by itself! That is quite amazing. That is because it is quality all the way. So if you are satisfied with just three you can just use the motherboard outputs: DVI, VGA, HDMI or Display Port. It does this through using the 4th and 5th Generation Core™

i7/i5/i3/Pentium®/Celeron® processors in the LGA1150 package, with iGPU, memory and PCI Express controllers integrated to support onboard graphics output with dedicated chipsets, 2-channel (4 DIMM) DDR3 memory and 16 PCI Express 3.0/2.0 lanes. This provides great graphics performance. Here is the back of the Sonata. Computer Monitors

The computer monitor is extremely important. Most new monitors are capable of outputting to DVI and VGA output. Some have HDMI or Display Port output. HDMI output is 1920 x 1080 pixels and that is what you see on most TVs. That is usually the best output for a normal 23 or a 24-inch trading monitor.

You are looking at your monitors all day long. Why not get the best monitors with the narrow thin bezels. It only makes since. Why go with old technology? All of trading computer manufactures wants you to buy their cheaper wide bezel monitors. They are doing a disservice to their customers!

We recommend and sell only the thin bezel type. This is the super thin edge, Asus monitor. Its screen size is 23.6". The response time is 1ms. The maximum resolution is 1920 x 1080. It is capable of being mounted on quad desk stands. It uses Splendid™ Video Intelligence Technology which optimizes video performance and image fidelity by enhancing color, brightness, contrast, and sharpness excellent for traders. Great for watching charts. These monitors can easily be attached to quad stands, which work nicely because of the thin edge. See the quad stand below.

Drives

The drives in the computer are important for performance. The new solid state drives are extremely fast. You can quickly see the difference in speed between a hard disk drive and a solid state drive. You'll never go back to a hard drive once you have experienced a solid state drive. The solid state drives are complicated devices and they actually regulate themselves to enhance their life. Memory locations in a SSD have only a limited amount of time it can be rewritten before it stops. The drive regulates itself to even out the wearing of any particular location. We use the Samsung solid state drives as their sustained sequential real and writes are over 500MB/s and life of these units are around 1,500,000 hours. We still use hard disk drives either for more drive space or as a 2nd drive or for backup. The most popular use we have for these is for cloning purposes using Acronis PC Backup and Recovery software. Many traders have us install an extra removable drive compartment on their computer. With these you can slide in a hard disk drive and clone the solid state drive with it. Then remove the drive and put it in a safe place. If anything happens to the solid state drive, like getting a virus on it, corruption or a failure, you can immediately put in the hard disk drive clone and boot from that and be up and running in a few minutes.

You can also copy the cloned drive over your corrupted solid state drive. You can also use the Acronis to do what is called continuous backup. That means that everything is backed up all the time.Speed of the Internet Internet speed is a major factor for traders. Most want the maximum speed possible. For most traders a bandwidth of 10GB is fine. You can go on the internet and check your speed.

For example go here:

http://www.speedtest.net

If you doing short term trades, for example, using one minute charts, you might want the fastest speed you can get, but for most 10GB is fine. The motherboard you use is also important to internet speed. The motherboard we use gives you high performance, prioritized bandwidth. It is called Turbo LAN. It uses Intel's Gigabit Ethernet and it both lowers demands on the processor and improves connection stability. It adds more support with Turbo LAN with cFosSpeed traffic shaping technology. Remote Go with total control anytime, anywhere

One of the motherboards we use allow you to gather ASUS Web Storage, Dropbox, Google Drive and Skydrive accounts in one place and backup to PC at the same time. You can easily access and control your PC anytime and anywhere.

Noise from Your Computer

Noise that your computer makes does really depend of the number of fans and their size and the quality of the fans. Most trading computer manufactures use cheap cases with low quality small fans. This is a serious problem because noise destroys your concentration to trade effectively. The noise comes from the CPU, video card and power supply fans. The quality of these parts and their fans makes the difference. The

Corsair power supplies and the Sonata case fans we use are noted for their quality and quietness. The CPU and case fans are optimizes for the lowest possible setting by the motherboard we use. Most other computers don't have this ability. Sonata Trading Computer Case The Sonata case uses minimalistic and stunning Scandinavian design fused with maximum sound reduction. The sides and front door panels are fitted with dense, sound-absorbing material making it a benchmark for noise reduction. It includes standard silent hydraulic bearing fans to keep internal components at optimal temperatures. The fans stay whisper quiet for daily use and extremely cool when trading. They are automatically controlled by the motherboard optimization. Trading Keyboard and Mouse

Sonata Keyboard

Having trouble seeing your keyboard? We recommend a backlit trading keyboard. If you are trading at night or in a dim light area you will want one of these.

Sonata Wireless Trading Mouse

Trading the markets, by drawing trend lines, angles, cycles and more on your computer, you are using you mouse constantly. You need a good mouse that fits your hand. The Sonata mouse has 2,500 DPI and has a blue LED light. The battery lasts up to 18 months. Comparable mice cost 4-times as much.

Operating System

We recommend Microsoft Windows 7 for the operating system. It comes in three different versions, the Home Premium, the Professional and the Ultimate. Most should get the Home Premium unless you want to use more than 16GB of memory. Then go with the Windows 7 Pro.

Anti-Virus Software

Anti-Virus software is an important consideration. You need a manufacture that keeps up with the various new viruses. You also want one that has excellent technical support in case you get a virus. Excellent customer service is very rate, nowadays, but this one has it. Also what I like is this software won't let you open a dangerous site to protect you from getting a virus. We highly recommend the TrendMicro Titanium Antivirus + Security.

Shipping Boxes

The shipping of a Trading Computer is important. Most manufactures don't know how to package a customized trading computer. They will put it in a box and put Styrofoam around it. The computer is usually then damaged at least 33% of the time. The problem is it is damaged in a way that is not really apparent. The damage could be to a motherboard, video card or power supply. The slight damage won't show up right away. It causes problems later on with failed parts. The Sonata is shipped in a special double box with double foam or Styrofoam support. The box has convenient handles for the shipping person to lift it easily and move it. Other manufactures use one box with no handles so the shipping person many times drops the box and causes damage. We have rarely any shipping damage to our computers and have used this special box to ship computers around the world with no damage whatsoever.

The Sonata Trading Computer

The Sonata is now such an amazing trading computer. It uses a one click, total system optimization system.

With this you get:

1) Robust overclocking

2) Energy savings

3) Digital power

4) Customized fan control

5) Tailored networking and audio settings.

Your trading computer is smart with this 5-way optimization. It dynamically optimizes essential aspects of your trading computer based on real-time use, so you get superb CPU performance, everyday energy savings, and ultra-stable digital power, cool and quiet fans and now even networking and audio settings that are tailored for the trading software you are using. In short, 5-way optimization ensures that your PC is perfect for trading, productivity or just about anything else! Trading Software runs swiftly and smoothly with high performance prioritized bandwidth and vivid sound. Fans stay whisper-quiet for everyday trading and ensures extreme cooling efficiency when trading Energy waste is reduced so you'll save money. Fans in the Sonata The computer scans each fan's characteristics and delivers a custom setting for each fan based on the dedicated area temperatures detected by hardware thermal sensors. The auto tuning mode scans fans parameters trough exclusive automatic speed detection to provide custom setting for each fan with a single click.

The Smoothest, slickest mouse controlled graphical BIOS is very appealing and helps you find your way quickly and easily. The BIOS has a special memory overclocking design. You can drive memory up to 3200 OC. Using T-Topology by minimizing the couple noise and signal reflection effect. Speed up you Sonata system with M.2., which supports up to 10Gbit/s. This is perfect for an operating system drive making your trading PC work much harder.

The difference between profit and loss can be measured in milliseconds. That why the Sonata motherboard are equipped with state-of-the-art networking technology that puts your speed first!

Turbo LAN with cFosSpeed traffic-shaping technology adds even more lag-reducing support and intuitive user interface. It allows you to lower lag in with no expert knowledge by up to 1.45! Just with a push of a button.

The Sonata CPU

The Sonata has Intel's latest CPU the Core i7-4790K Quad Core 4.GHz. It is a big improvement over the i7-3770K. This is the fastest stock speed CPU that Intel has ever released to consumers.

The flawless audio that the Sonata has helps to make you part of a chat room for trading, if you belong to one. It makes short work of optimizing audio settings for the way you want to listen. Intel Gigabit Ethernet – gives you faster internet speed. It is much better and smoother for trading. It has the serious double advantage of communicating directly with CPUs and offering high

TCP and UDP throughput. The Sonata works with up to 3 displays right out of the motherboard. I have never seen this before. This is quite amazing.

The Graphic Card

The GT640- DCSL-2GD3 is the graphics card we use in the Sonata. Each card supports 4 monitors or with 2 cards supports 8 monitors. Gives you direct connect heat pipes and lowers temps by 16% with zero noise. Pumps up graphic performance with super alloy power delivering a 15% performance boost. Dust proof fan design increases particle resistance and extends card life.

Solid State Drives

The Sonata is significantly faster than a computer with a standard HDD, providing more sequential and random read write times for every trading task using Samsung Solid State drives. The drive stores data more efficiently increasing both speed and reliability.

Upgrades

If you already have a Sonata Trading Computer, you can in many cases upgrade it to the latest technology for usually $700.00 - $800.00. If you have Microsoft Windows XP you will also want to upgrade that to Windows 7. You will need the original box and outer box to return the computer.

Get Your Sonata Trading Computer for FREE!

When You Open a New Account with TradeStation Securities Yes, you can get TradeStation's fantastic trading platform, which has won many awards. You also can get Radar Screen and Portfolio Maestro for FREE the first month (a value of $159.00) as well as 1st $500 in Commissions Cash Back. After the 1st $500.00 is credited then TradeStation will pay you 20% cash back on commissions each month until your Sonata Trading Computer is paid for up to $8000.00! The Value of this Trading Computer Deal is $8700.00! There is a $5000.00 minimum account size and can include even an IRA too. (Forex is not included).

If you do have a TradeSation account this, you can still make this deal if you open a new TradeStation second account. Also a new futures client can also receive a reduced data package for only $20.00 a month, which includes the real time data for all electronic contracts traded on the CME, CBOT, NYMEX and COMEX. This $20.00 fee will be for the life of their futures account.

CME $70.00

CBOT $70.00

NYMEX $70.00

COMEX $70.00

Total Monthly Charges $280.00.

That adds up to a year charge for exchange fees of $3360.00 You would only pay $20.00 per month or $240.00 per year That saves you $3120.00 per year off of exchange fees on top of the commission rebate and discounts you are getting that basically pays for your computer!

CALL Kevin Myslinski AT TRADESTATION – 888-223-9658 to open your account or if you have specific Tradestation questions. This promo is subject to change or end at any time.

Larry Jacobs
tradersworld@gmail.com
Halliker's, Inc.
www.SonataTradingComputer.com

Chapter 17 - Mastering the Emotions of Trading to Build a Peak Performance Trading Mind by Rande Howell

Everyone has seen it happen. Something snaps and knowledgeable traders start falling apart and blowing it in the heat of trading. You probably have experienced it personally more than once. Retail traders and professional traders usually have different routes to the failure of their highly trained minds. But on the P&L statement of both – it shows up red.

The retail trader usually comes to the game of trading with a lack of tolerance for risking capital (expressed as a need for control over outcome) and believes ardently that superior knowledge is all he needs to win. Meanwhile, the professional trader sooner or later gets ambushed by euphoric over-confidence (irrational exuberance) and mismanages risk till it bites him hard. Euphoria smashed by serious threatening consequences, the memory of those losses then begins to foreshadow his calculation of entries. It's hard to shake once the trauma of losses become real. Either way, both the retail and the professional traders end up with compromised minds at the very moment they need their A-game to perform.

This cycle is the never ending story of both Main Street traders and Wall Street traders. At least until the trader begins to wise up to the "head game" aspect of trading. It is this inner game of trading that separates the wheat from the chaff. Mere knowledge versus performance-tested knowledge – being able to act coolly under pressure. And not being seduced either by fear's irrational pessimism or by euphoria's over-confidence and irrational exuberance.

This need for emotional state management is what we examined in last month's article, The Emotions of Money and Loss. There the necessity of calming (regulating) emotions was addressed before they could compromise your trading mind. Once the mind has been hijacked by emotions – it's too late. The damage is done. But let's say that you have learned to regulate emotions so that you are not being sucked into the vortex of either irrational pessimism or irrational exuberance (the two horsemen of the trading apocalypse) - what happens then?

The Mind in Conflict You Never Thought You Had

Let's say you have succeeded in calming your emotions. What does that get you? It gets you to the door of the mind. It is here where you need to step back for a moment and ask the question, "What is the mind, anyway?" Most likely your perception is that the mind is where "your" thoughts take place. Just "you" and "your" thoughts. How could it be more complicated than that?

Let's re-think mind so that you have a different, and more effective, way of understanding of what, exactly, is going on in your head as you trade, when you get out of your comfort zone. Have you ever really noticed your thoughts while you are trading? Have you noticed that a heated and spirited debate often breaks out in your head when making a trading decision? Suddenly, "you" are of two minds, or more. It's like a tug of war going on inside your head. There are at least two sides (actually a good bit more as you will come to learn) in competition to win the argument. So now "your" thoughts are divided into two armed camps (or more) trying to control the direction of decision making – of what you are going to do.

This is where the trader gets in trouble. Often, the voice of reason gets pushed aside during the conflict going on inside your head. Imagine, here you are in the thick of the moment, and reason (what you need most to trade effectively) is no longer heard over the cacophony ramping up to an emotional meltdown. Reason, drowned out by louder voices, results in reactive emotional thinking taking over the mind.

What and who are these other voices trying to get control over your decision making under pressure? Until you stop to notice the debate going on in your head, it just passes beneath the radar of your awareness. And in this mindlessness of what is happening right under your nose, you stay stuck in the self-limiting patterns that negatively impact long term trading performance.

You can deny that this internal struggle goes on consistently in your mind, but you can't deny the consequences (drawdowns in your trading account) of denying this reality. It's your turning a blind eye to this internal struggle that keeps you stuck in self-limiting patterns. Whether or not your problems are at trade entry, trade management, or exiting trades (beating yourself up for losing), you will find a raging debate going on beneath the surface of your awareness. Sometimes that debate is of a judgmental or critical nature and sometimes it is euphoric in its temptation to throw prudent risk control to the wind, but the fact remains that your mind is engaged in a heated debate about managing the uncertainty about future consequences with which you are forced to deal.

This is where the biology of the brain intersects with the psychology of the mind. Since the mind emerges from the brain – let's take a look at your trading brain/mind.

It's a Crowded Place Inside Your Head

To David Eagleman (an eminent neuro-scientist and author) the brain is a community of rival programs "duking it out" for control of the adaptive forces in the brain. These rival programs are emotional in nature and are seeking your short term survival. They seek control of outcome – survival in the moment. They do not have the capacity to think long term (to manage probability). Once a coalition of these emotional programs, embedded into neuro-circuits, wins the battle of survival dominance, their reactive patterns BEGIN TO MAKE YOU. This is what you are experiencing in the heated debates in your head while you are trying to make trading decisions - the probability of long term gain in your trading decisions versus the short term survival patterns that have become powerful and reactive.

David Rosenbaum (another eminent neuro-scientist) takes it even a step further. He asserts that the brain is a jungle (occupied by all sorts of critters) governed by Darwinian laws of competition and cooperation. There lies the rivalry of competition and also the cooperation of team building that ultimately form the brain/mind that you bring to trading. Now let's take it one step further.

When the mind emerges from this community of rival programs called the brain, the programs of the brain are given voice as thoughts in your mind. So "your" thoughts are the product of various emotional programs that have established control over other emotional programs and are given voice in the thoughts of your mind. Except for the "rational" program (which is not one of the primitive emotional programs), all have a bias for short term survival.

And in your lack of understanding of the brain/mind, you have come to believe (by default) that a particular organization of these programs given voice in your mind REALLY IS "YOU". Until these more primitive programs can be understood and regulated, there is very little chance that the "rational" program – or the Sage Archetype – will seize the control of the thinking mind and trade successfully for the long term. And this is why people continue to fail at trading when they, in fact, know how to trade. They cannot get the rational program on line (and maintain order) in the heat of stress. To do that, you are going to need to come to a new understanding of the forces that make up the mind and you are going to have to learn how to observe these forces.

Activating the Dormant Skill of Observation

Have you ever been stressed to the point of not being able to think straight and taken a break (i.e. a walk, a weekend getaway, or talking to a trusted confidante) and come back with a fresh perspective on the problem that was giving you so much trouble? Of course you have. What you may not realize is that, unbeknownst to you, the talent of mindfulness was activated. And in that moment of calm, you were able to re-organize your thinking. Moving that raw talent into a refined skill is essential for rebuilding the mind for trading.

Stepping back out of the situation for a moment allowed you to see the problem from a less cluttered observation point. This is mindfulness, or awakening the observing self. And it can be developed as a skill so that you don't have to physically step out of a situation to see the situation differently. Instead, you develop the skill of detaching yourself from the comings and goings of your thought life and begin questioning (examining) the evidence from which an assessment springs. This way, you no longer get ambushed by emotional hijackings and can choose which mind you bring to the management of uncertainty that defines your trading success.

As you begin to really practice this mindfulness, you discover that many of the unquestioned "truths" running around your head (i.e. declaring the sky is falling or that there is gold at the end of the rainbow) that urge immediate action have no grounding in fact. It's humbling for a trader to come to grips with this. This is because, while under pressure, he or she has been acting on ungrounded assessments masquerading as irrevocable truths. This is what happens when you calm the emotions down through emotional regulation (which is essential) and see your thoughts through the lens of observation.

Suddenly you, the trader, begins to see that old established emotional programs in the brain have been given unfettered access to the decisions of your trading mind. These old emotional programs, given voice in your thoughts, were probably successful in another time and place where they adapted you for survival. But in the here and now of trading, where probability-based (rather than reactive survival-based) thinking is essential for long-term success, they are an artifact of an earlier mind that is no longer relevant in the brave new world of trading.

As a start for awakening the observer and becoming mindful, I invite you to keep a specific journal of your trades. Start and focus on the internal debates you have at critical times. Ask these questions of the voices in the argument:

1. What is the thought saying?

2. What emotion is attached to the thought? (All thinking is emotional state dependent.)

3. What is the evidence that supports its assessment?

4. Is it true as a fact or is it only an assessment that may or may not be grounded in evidence?

5. Is the thought trying to help you or hinder your progress as a trader?

6. What happens to the voice of the thought as you un-fuse with it and examine it?

The survival part of your brain is always going to want to control outcome – even if it is only an illusion. The brain/mind, for trading success, is going to have to be reorganized around the one thing it can control – your performance of execution. The outcome of a trade cannot be controlled, but the mind can be organized to control its performance – that is the peak performance edge. Next month, we will take a closer look at the community of the mind. We will learn who the players are and what their intentions are. Remember, it's a jungle in there waiting to be cultivated - if you have the eyes to see and discern.

Rande Howell
rande.howell@tradersstateofmind.com

Traders State of Mind
www.tradersstateofmind.com

Chapter 18- Trading the FOMC Sessions with Precision by Mohan

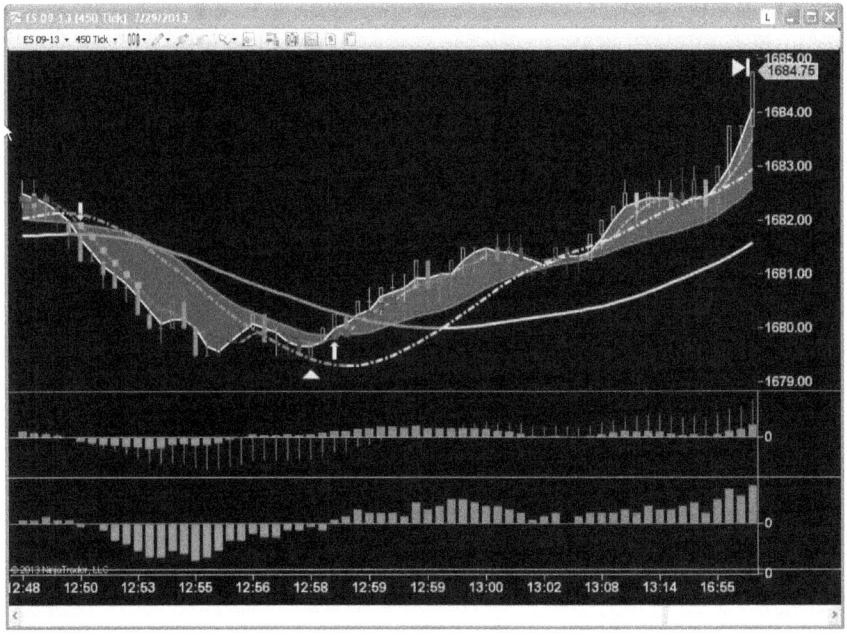

On Tuesday and Wednesday of this week (January 28th and 29th) the FOMC meeting got started. These meetings are a regular monthly occurrence that can greatly affect the markets.

Often during the FOMC meetings it is best to stand aside after the first 2-3 hours of trading as the announcement time approaches at 2:00 est.

On specific FOMC session announcement days where the release is about the "interest rates" the market can show very volatile price swings. Usually there is a scheduled press conference after these sessions which can add to the market fluctuations.

Usually after the initial whip saw from the announcement the market will try to stabilize. This usually occurs during the press conference and then often a directional move will occur after the range bound period.

These can be very difficult sessions to trade but if you have the correct tools and knowledge to trade the FOMC announcement days it can be very profitable too.

Note how in the short 5 minute video below I go over all of the Boomerang trade setups and how an astute trader using Boomerang could have had a long string of winning trades during this 2 day period.

I know the review runs a bit fast as I am showing 2 days of setups in just 5 minutes. For more details in a slow analysis be sure to attend our webinars.

I invite you to seriously study this video and others in our library and take your trading to the next level.

Boomerang Day Trader is one of the top day trading software in the industry and the lowest cost. Most of our sales come from referrals by traders who are already successfully navigating the markets with Boomerang. Join us and start making steady, consistent winning trades.

Here is today's video tutorial:

http://www.screencast.com/t/Ql7QrYcmzZlg

Take a look at this recent Video Tutorial below which shows 14 crystal clear winning Boomerang Day Trader setups in a row and no stop outs. This is a new record for Boomerang Day Trader!

http://www.screencast.com/t/WLT2kLeLxHp

If you would like a copy of our exact Boomerang Day Trader simple Method/Rules to follow along on the webinars or video tutorials email me at : mohan@daytradersaction.com

Each month we have two webinars for our free training for Boomerang owners. You are welcome to attend these webinars before you purchase BDT. These will be more informal type of webinars where I spend time going over Insights into trading with Boomerang Day Trader and answering your questions.

If you are just learning about Boomerang Day Trader this is a chance to see the full Boomerang charts and the One Core Trade Setup that we use to show the excellent returns that are posted on the blog at www.boomerangtrader.com

Mohan
mohan@daytradersaction.com
Day Traders Action, Inc.
www.daytradersaction.com

CHAPTER 19- LINKS TO PRESENTATIONS

These links will only work for a short period of time. You can go to http://www.tradersworldonlineexpo.com at a later date for these and hundreds of other video trading links. During the expos the links are free. Later on you need to be a member of TradersWorld.

Steve Wheeler - Secrets To Making Money Everyday

Tim Bost - What Really Works to GIve You More Success in the Markets

Mohan - How to trade the market with extreme precision using Boomerang Day Trader

Jaime Johnson - Multiple Unit and Time Frame FOREX Strategies for Current Market Positions

Bennett McDowell - The Benefits of One-On-One Coaching

Lars von Thienen - How dominant cycles of "financial stress" can pinpoint market turns

Thomas Barmann - Learn to Trade It's Never Too Late

David Choe - Finding the Perfect Trade Setup

Al McWhirr - The EminiScalp ABL Auto Trade Strategy

John Matteson - The Cyclical Nature of Trading

Gail Mercer - Why Do Traders Love Nadex Binary Options?

Barry Burns - "Simple Tips to Dramatically Improve Your Trading Discipline, Remove Fear and Hesitation, and Trade with Confidence and Consistency."

Robert Miner - Multiple Time Frame Trade Strategies

Steven Primo - The 1 Chart Pattern That Can Make You Successful

John Karnas - TrendFollowingTrades Releases the New Discretionary UltimateV1 Indicators

Jim McQuarrie - Trading and staying off the crazy cycle

Adrienne Toghraie - All About Losses

Larry Jacobs - Sonata Trading Computer

Rande Howell - Mastering Your Emotions to Create a Peak Performance Trading Mind

Tom Alexander - The Essence of Market Profile: Auction Market Principles

Sean Mckissen - x3 Futures Day Trading System

Copyright

Copyright 2014 Halliker's, Inc., All rights reserved. Information in this publication must not be reproduced in any form without written permission from the publisher. Traders World Digest is published quarterly by Halliker's, Inc., 2508 W. Grayrock Dr., Springfield, MO 65810. Created in the U.S.A. is prepared from information believed to be reliable but not guaranteed us without further verification and does not purport to be complete. Futures and options trading are speculative and involve risk of loss.

Disclaimer

Risk Disclaimer:

All trading involves risk. Leveraged trading has large potential rewards, but also large potential risk. Be aware and accept this risk before trading. Never trade with money you cannot afford to lose. All forecasting is based on past performance and past performance of any trading methodology is no guarantee of future results. No "safe" trading system has ever been devised and no one can guarantee profits or freedom from loss. No representation is being made that any account will achieve profits or losses similar to those discussed. There is no guarantee that, even with the best advice available, you will become a successful trader because not everyone has what it takes to be a successful trader. The trading strategies discussed may be unsuitable for you depending upon your specific investment objectives and financial position. You must make your own investment decisions in light of your own investment objectives, risk profile, and circumstances. Use independent advisors as you believe necessary. Therefore, the information provided herein is not intended to be specific advice as to whether you should engage in a particular trading strategy or buy, sell, or hold any financial product. Margin requirements, tax considerations, commissions, and other transaction costs may significantly affect the economic consequences of the trading strategies or transactions discussed and you should review such requirements with your own legal, tax and financial advisors. Before engaging in such trading activities, you should understand the nature and extent of your rights and obligations and be aware of the risks involved. All testimonials are unsolicited and are potentially non-representative of all clients. Halliker's,Inc. dba Traders World is not a broker or licensed investment advisor and therefore is not licensed to tailor general investment advice for individual traders. Your actions and the results of your actions in regard to anything you receive from Halliker's,Inc. dba Traders World or any of our writers or presenters are entirely your own responsibility. Halliker's,Inc. dba Traders World or any of the writers or presenters cannot and will not assume liability for any losses that may be incurred by the use of any information received from Halliker's,Inc. dba Traders World or any of the writers or presenters of the expos. Any such liability is hereby expressly disclaimed.

Hypothetical Disclaimer: All results are considered to be Hypothetical: Hypothetical performance results have many inherent limitations. Unlike an actual performance record, simulated results do not represent actual trading. Also, since the trades have not actually been executed, the results may have under or over compensated for the impact, if any, of certain market factors, such as lack of liquidity. No representation is being made that any account will or is likely to achieve profits or losses similar to those shown. In fact, there are frequently sharp differences between hypothetical performance results and the actual results subsequently achieved by any particular trading program. Furthermore, only risk capital should be used for leveraged trading due to the high risk of loss involved. One of the limitations of hypothetical performance results is that they are generally prepared with the benefit of hindsight. In addition, hypothetical trading does not involve financial risk, and no hypothetical trading record can completely account for the impact of financial risk in actual trading. For example, the ability to withstand losses (and incur account drawdowns) or to adhere to a particular trading program in spite of trading loses are important issues which can also adversely affect actual trading results. There are numerous other factors related to the markets in general or to the implementation of any specific trading program, method or system, which cannot be completely taken into consideration with hypothetical performance results and will affect trading results and your P/L.

Trading Disclaimer:

Futures and forex trading have large potential rewards, but also large potential risk. You must be aware of the risks and be willing to accept them in order to invest in the futures and options markets. Don't trade with money you can't afford to lose. This letter is neither a solicitation nor an offer to Buy/Sell futures or options. No representation is being made that any account will or is likely to achieve profits or losses similar to those discussed on this letter. The past performance of any trading system or methodology is not necessarily indicative of future results. Trading foreign currencies is a challenging and potentially profitable opportunity for educated and experienced investors. However, before deciding to participate in the Forex market, you should carefully consider your investment objectives, level of experience and risk appetite. Most importantly, do not invest money you cannot afford to lose. There is considerable exposure to risk in any foreign exchange transaction. Any transaction involving currencies involves risks including, but not limited to, the potential for changing political and/or economic conditions that may substantially affect the price or liquidity of a currency.

CFTC RULE 4.41 - HYPOTHETICAL OR SIMULATED PERFORMANCE RESULTS HAVE CERTAIN LIMITATIONS. UNLIKE AN ACTUAL PERFORMANCE RECORD, SIMULATED RESULTS DO NOT REPRESENT ACTUAL TRADING. ALSO, SINCE THE TRADES HAVE NOT BEEN EXECUTED, THE RESULTS MAY HAVE UNDER- OR-OVER COMPENSATED FOR THE IMPACT, IF ANY, OF CERTAIN MARKET FACTORS, SUCH AS LACK OF LIQUIDITY. SIMULATED TRADING PROGRAMS IN GENERAL ARE ALSO SUBJECT TO THE FACT THAT THEY ARE DESIGNED WITH THE BENEFIT OF HINDSIGHT. NO REPRESENTATION IS BEING MADE THAT ANY ACCOUNT WILL OR IS LIKELY TO ACHIEVE PROFIT OR LOSSES SIMILAR TO THOSE SHOWN.

No representation is being made that any account will or is likely to achieve profits or losses similar to those shown. In fact, there are frequently sharp differences between hypothetical performance results and the actual results subsequently achieved by any particular trading program. Hypothetical trading does not involve financial risk, and no hypothetical trading record can completely account for the impact of financial risk in actual trading.

About The Authors

[name] = Steve Wheeler

[email] = Support@navitrader.com

[Company] = NaviTrader

[Website] = www.navitrader.com

[Phone] = 800-987-6269

[Background] = Steve trades in the stock/options/futures and FOREX markets. He has been actively trading for the past 25 years. He developed the Trendicator & TradeFinder charts that are used by thousands of discretionary traders around the world. He has authored many publications on trading including Financial Independence through Trading Stocks, Options & Futures. He speaks nationally/internationally to trading groups. He is an honors graduate from University of WI & graduate school at the University of MN. He was a CPA before becoming a full-time Trader.

[name] = Tim Bost

[email] = tim@timbost.com

[Company] = Financial Cycles Weekly

[Website] = www.FinancialCyclesWeekly.com

[Phone] = 941-351-2888

[Background] = Tim Bost is the author of over 2 dozen books and monographs on market strategies, market cycles and astro-trading, including "Mercury, Money and the Markets" and "Gann Secrets Revealed: Beyond Symolism in Financial Astrology" Since 1988 he has published FinancialCyclesWeekly.com newsletter, an internationally-circulated publication providing market forecasts and analysis, educational materials for astro-traders, and a Model Portfolio with an 11-year record of consistent market out-performance.

[name] = Mohan

[email] = mohan@daytradersaction.com

[Company] = Day Traders Action, Inc.

[Website] = www.daytradersaction.com

[Phone] = (877) 810-5561

[Background] = I have been trading the futures markets for 25 years since the crash of 1987. We have been assisting thousands of traders for 14 years in the trading community through "Mohan's Precision Trading Services". My "Daily Directional Forecast" newsletter is the first of its kind telling subscribers exactly where the market is going each day...before the opening bell. We also offer one of the top selling day trading software on NinjaTrader called "Boomerang Day Trader".

[name] = Jaime Johnson

[email] = jaime@nobsfxtrading.com

[Company] = NoBSFX Trading.

[Website] = www.nobsfx.com

[Phone] = (760) 536-4171

[Background] = I was trained by my mentor Robert Miner of Dynamic Traders Group and have been an active FOREX, Stock and ETF Trader since 2000 and the Chief Trade Strategist for Dynamic Traders Group since 2003. I have written numerous articles for top trading magazines and educational material teaching my analysis and trade strategies I use in my educational material as well as my own trading. I am now the president of NoBSFX Trading continuing my analysis and trade strategies I use on a daily basis with a focus on the top FOREX markets.

[name] = Bennett McDowell

[email] = bennett@traderscoach.com

[Company] = TradersCoach.com

[Website] = www.traderscoach.com

[Phone] = 858-695-0592

[Background] = Techncial Analysis

[name] = Lars von Thienen

[email] = whentotradeinfo@gmail.com

[Company] = WhenToTrade

[Website] = www.whentotrade.com

[Phone] =

[Background] = Trader, Engineer and Consultant

[name] = Thomas Barrman

[email] = contact@NeverLossTrading.com

[Company] = NeverLossTrading

[Website] = www.NeverLossTrading.com

[Phone] = 866-455-4520

[Background] = President

[Background] = Owner and Inventor of NeverLossTrading® and TradeColors.com Author of the Book: "My Stock Market Income" and "Your Trading Career as a Private Investor" His first introduction to trading came when he was 22 years old (31 years ago). Over the years, he acquired a wealth of knowledge, how private investors can make money in the markets by focusing on constant income instead of growth. He trades by taking advantage of spotting and trading institutional price moves, minimizing risk and compounding interest. His aim is to make the world a better place by sharing knowledge and giving education. A very small group of people keeps the knowledge how to trade the financial markets and those who enter, without being well prepared, mostly donate their hard-earned money to those who know. NeverLossTrading® and TradeColors.com are easy to follow, market proven trading and investing concepts he is sharing with you.

Thomas is the author of two books and many publications: My Stock Market Income and Your Trading Career as a Private Investor

[name] = David Choe

[email] = choesen@hotmail.com

[Company] = Choesen Trade LLC

[Website] = CandlestickFigures.com

[Phone] =

[Background] = Hi, I've been a trader for about 8 years who trades purely based on technicals. The timeframes I prefer to trade are mostly for day trading and swing trading using candlesticks. As I began my trading journey, I would spend countless hours researching stock charts trying to find the perfect setups. I began to notice certain candlestick setups would repeat consistently on multiple timeframes, but they weren't your usual traditional candlestick patterns. They were slight variations of patterns which I could not find using any other candlestick scanner that you could get online or that came with your trading platforms. That's when I decided to develop my own software that is a customizable candlestick software to create and find any setup I choose to design. This allowed me to find the perfect setups and start my first business at the same time.

[name] = Al McWhirr

[email] = al.mcwhirr@verizon.net

[Company] = EminiScalp.com

[Website] = www.eminiscalp.com

[Phone] = 201-768-3520

[Background] = Managing Partner of EminiScalp.com. Retired high school teacher of 41 years. Adjunct college professor for 20 years. Past President and executive board member of the New Jersey Cooperative Education Coordinators Association Education. NJCIECA Coordinator Of The Year honors. Author of Day Trading Turmoil To Triumph.

[name] = John Matteson

[email] = scalpersgold@yahoo.com

[Company] = MTPredictor

[Website] = www.mtpredictor.us

[Phone] = 407-566-1373

[Background] = 1996 Investment Specialist Charles Schwab, 2002 full-time day trader, multiple franchise owner, real estate investor, 2007 Trader of the Year, 2010 graduate of the Online Trading Academy, 2013 contributed to the Kindle best seller, "Learn the Secrets of Successful Traders".

[name] = Gail Mercer

[email] = tradersworld@gmail.com

[Company] = Traders Help Desk

[Website] = www.TradersHelpDesk.com

[Phone] = 336 328-8848

[Background] = President

[name] = Barry Burns

[email] = mmentors@hotmail.com

[Company] = Top Dog Trading

[Website] = www.topdogtrading.com

[Phone] = 951-515-8515

[Background] = Dr. Barry Burns is the author of "Trend Trading For Dummies" (Pulisher: Wiley and sons, 2014), has been a seminar presenter for several exchanges including the CME Group and Eurex, received Readers Choice Awards for "Technical Anaysis Web Sites" and "Trading Schools" by Technical Analysis of Stocks and Commodities Magazine, and founded TopDogTrading.com to help traders shorten their learning curve in becoming successful.

[name] = Robert Miner

[email] = bob@dynamictraders.com

[Company] = Dynamic Traders Group, Inc.

[Website] = www.DynamicTraders.com

[Phone] = 9708190121

[Background] = Trader, publisher since 1984

[name] = Steven Primo

[email] = stevenprimo@specialisttrading.com

[Company] = Specialist Trading

[Website] = www.specialisttrading.com

[Phone] = 310-844-7220

[Background] = President and Founder

[name] = John Karnas

[email] = john.karnas@verizon.net

[Company] = Trend Following Trades, LLC.

[Website] = Trendfollowingtrades.com

[Phone] = 215-909-9617

[Background] = Owner/Trader/Educator

Jim McQuarrie

[email] jamthetrader@gmail.com

[Company] = Sites By JAM

[Website] = www.strategicdaytrading.com

[Phone] = 888-477-1115

[Background] = I have been trading for 20 years and teaching for 8

[name] = Adrienne Toghraie, Trader's Success Coach

[email] = Adrienne@TradingOnTarget.com

[Company] = TradingOnTarget.com

[Website] = TradingOnTarget.com

[Phone] = 919-851-8288

[Background] = Trader's Success Coach - 24 years in the business of coaching and mentoring traders to higher levels of performance. I have written 15 published books and have been a keynote speaker at most of the major trading conferences.

[name] = Larry Jacobs

[email] = tradersworld@gmail.com

[Company] = Halliker's, Inc.

[Website] = www.SonataTradingComputer.com

[Phone] = 417-882-9697

[Background] = President

[Background] = Larry Jacobs has a BS and Masters Degree in Business. He started in the financial industry as a stock and futures broker in a major brokerage company in 1976 and was a broker for 24 years. He started a financial magazine in 1978, " The Gann & Elliott Wave Magazine" which was later changed in name to "Traders World Magazine". www.tradersworld.com The magazine is quarterly and is distributed to book stores across the United States and Canada and to subscribers across the world. 12,000 issues are distributed quarterly. He also created the Sonata Trading Computer division, which is built and is optimized specifically for trading for speed and reliability.www.sonatatradingcomputers.com. The computer has been sold to traders in almost every state in the United States and many foreign countries. He has author of seven trading books: Gann Masters, Gann Masters II, How to Make Time and Price

Overlays, Gann Masters Charts Unveiled, W.D. Gann in Real-Time Trading, Patterns & Ellipses, Elliott Wave Masters

Won first place in the Robbins World Cup Trading Championship 2001 (Stock Division).
Won third place in the Robbins World Cup Trading Championship 2000 (Stock Division).

[name] = Rande Howell

[email] = rande.howell@tradersstateofmind.com

[Company] = Traders State of Mind

[Website] = www.tradersstateofmind.com

[Phone] = 704.996.8438

[Background] = Rande Howell is both a licensed therapist and a performance coach. He teaches traders how to manage their emotions so that they can master the head game of trading. His work is rooted in Emotional Intelligence and Mindfulness and teaches how to harness your emotional nature for success.

[name] = Tom Alexander

[email] = tom@alexandertrading.com

[Company] = Alexander Trading

[Website] = www.alexandertrading.com

[Phone] = 912-401-8617

[Background] = 30 years trading: Private trader, institutional trader, trading educator and consultant for past 10 years.

[name] = Sean Mckissen

[email] = mckissen333@yahoo.com

[Company] = 360Wallst

[Website] = http://www.360wallst.com/

[Phone] = 2096691190

[Background] = Sean has 20 years of trading experience trading stocks, options and futures. In the past Sean was the branch manager of VIP futures with clients all over the world. Now the focus is to help individual traders achieve their trading goals with very specific trading systems and rules. Over the years Sean has built many systems over the years and is now releasing the most specific futures day trading system on the market.

www.ingramcontent.com/pod-product-compliance
Lightning Source LLC
Chambersburg PA
CBHW051643170526
45167CB00001B/316